PAUL SÉDIR

Dreams & Letters

DREAMS: THEORIES–PRACTICE–INTERPRETATION
First published as *Les Rêves. Théories, pratique, interprétation*,
Beaudelot, 1900

MAGIC LETTERS
First published as *Lettres magiques - Roman d'initiations orientales*,
Ollendorff, 1901

PAUL SÉDIR

ISBN 978-1-914166-24-2 (HB)
ISBN 978-1-914166-25-9 (PB)

Hardcover edition printed by Biddles, Norfolk.
First published in 2023.
Hadean Press Limited
59a Cavendish Street
Keighley, West Yorkshire
BD21 3RB
www.hadeanpress.com

PAUL SÉDIR

DREAMS

Theory — Practice — Interpretation

&

MAGIC LETTERS

Historical Biography and English Translation

by

AUSTIN J. AVISON

Pictured right:. Paul Sédir, pseudonym of Yvon Le Loup (1871-1926), was a French author, mystic, kabbalist, Rosicrucian, and Martinist.

Contents

ꟾNTRODUCTION

Paul Sédir, or Sédir (originally Yvon Le Loup, 2 January 1871 – 3 February 1926), emerged as a pivotal figure in the scholarly discourse on French esotericism and Christian mysticism in the early 20th century. His extensive scholarly output not only marks a critical phase in the evolution of French esoteric thought but also bridges a significant gap between academic and mystical understandings of the esoteric realm. Born into the family of Hippolyte Le Loup and Séraphine Foeller in Dinan, Brittany, and later relocating to Paris, Sédir demonstrated an early inclination towards the arcane, particularly in the fields of Kabbalah and alchemy. Embarking on a dual career path in 1892 at the Banque de France, Sédir concurrently pursued an in-depth study of esotericism. His intellectual pursuits led him to explore and articulate the intricate nuances of metaphysical and mystical dimensions, which he perceived as subtly interwoven with the fabric of conscious reality, accessible to those attuned to its presence.

Sédir's first text, *Les Miroirs Magiques* (*Magic Mirrors*), was published in 1894 by Lucien Chamuel. This work, along with others like *Les Tempéraments et la Culture psychique* (1894), *Les Incantations* (1897), and *La Médecine occulte* (1900), reflects his profound knowledge in various domains of esotericism, including Kabbalah, astral light, and magical practices. His works often combined scientific botany with esoteric herbalism, as seen in *Les Plantes magiques* (1902), which delved into the occult properties of plants and their medico-magical uses. Sédir's legacy is marked by his initial contributions to esoteric literature and his eventual advocacy for a more direct, spiritual approach to understanding the divine, devoid of esoteric practices and initiations. This change in perspective, particularly his critique of Martinism as 'eclectic and antichristic', reveals his deep commitment to seeking truth, a journey that ultimately led him to embrace Christian spirituality over esotericism.

Sédir met Dr. Gérard Anaclet Vincent Encausse (1865 – 1916), i.e., Papus, at the Librairie du Merveilleux bookshop in 1889. This bookshop, established by Lucien Chamuel, was more than a store: it was a focal point for esoteric gatherings, publishing, and conferences. Sédir, deeply interested in esotericism, quickly formed a close bond with Papus, who provided him access to a vast array of literature on symbolism, philosophy, and esotericism. Sédir's eagerness for knowledge led him to collaborate with Papus, contributing articles to Papus' magazine *Le Voile d'Isis*, and being initiated into the Martinist Order, where he reached the position of Superior Unknown Initiator and became a member of the Supreme Council before leaving the Order in 1910. Their close friendship and collaboration revolved around a shared passion for Kabbalah, alchemy, and other esoteric traditions, with Sédir rapidly becoming one of Papus' most trusted allies (Sédir, 1900; Sédir, 1908, p. 10).

Papus led the revival of Western esotericism

and spent much of his early life studying subjects such
as Kabbalah, occult tarot, magic, alchemy, and the
works of Eliphas Lévi at the Bibliothèque Nationale
(Goodrick-Clarke, 2008, p. 145). He was initially a
member of the French Theosophical Society but
resigned due to its focus on Eastern occultism. Papus
co-founded the Kabbalistic Order of the Rose-Croix
in 1888 and was involved in various esoteric and
paramasonic organizations. He balanced his esoteric
pursuits with conventional academic studies, earning
a Doctor of Medicine degree from the University of
Paris in 1894. Papus also played a significant role as
a physician and occult consultant to Tsar Nicholas II
and Tsarina Alexandra of Russia, advising them on
numerous occasions against their reliance on occultism
for government decisions.

Papus emerged as a central figure in the
resurgence of Western esotericism during the late 19th
and early 20th centuries. His initiation into the realms of
occultism commenced under the guidance of Marquis
Joseph Alexandre Saint-Yves d'Alveydre, a significant
mentor who facilitated Papus' introduction to Stanislas
de Guaita. This partnership was instrumental in the
establishment of the Kabbalistic Order of the Rose-
Croix, a seminal organization in esoteric circles.

Papus' intellectual pursuits were profoundly
influenced by Éliphas Lévi, particularly his translation
of the *Nuctemeron* of Apollonius of Tyana, which
directly inspired Papus' nom de plume. Additionally,
Papus engaged extensively with the philosophical
corpus of Louis Claude de Saint-Martin (1743 –

1803), the revered French mystic colloquially known as 'the unknown philosopher'. This engagement was a catalyst for Papus' revitalization of the Martinist Order in 1891, an order devoted to the principles of Hermeticism and asserting a spiritual lineage originating from Saint-Martin himself (Sédir, 1908, p. 10; Goodrick-Clarke, 2008, p. 145; 196).

Beyond the re-establishment of the Martinist Order, Papus' contributions to esotericism were multifaceted. He purportedly held original documents from Martinez de Pasqually and assumed a significant role in the Rite of Saint-Martin. Furthermore, Papus was instrumental in the advancement of the Hermes branch of the Theosophical Society of Paris, founded in 1887 (Goodrick-Clarke, 2008, p. 145; 196). His influence extended to ecclesiastical roles, notably his consecration as a bishop within the Gnostic Church of France and his involvement with the Hermetic Order of the Golden Dawn in Paris. Notably, Papus founded the O.T.O. Gnostic Catholic Church, aligning with the tradition of French Neo-Gnosticism, and succeeded John Yarker as the Grand Hierophant of the Ancient and Primitive Rite of Memphis and Mizraim.

Martinism, an 18th-century French Christian esoteric movement, was profoundly influenced by the teachings of Louis-Claude de Saint-Martin and the theurgical and Kabbalistic insights of Martines de Pasqually. Jacques de Livron Joachim de la Tour de la Casa Martinez de Pasqually, a mysterious figure in the world of theosophy, established the Order of Knight-Masons Elect Priests of the Universe, also known as the Elus Cohens, in 1761. This Order played a pivotal role in the spiritual development of both Saint-Martin and Jean-Baptiste Willermoz, serving as a foundation for their later contributions to Martinism.

The roots of Martinism trace back to the mid-18th century, anchored in the mystical and theurgical works of Martinez de Pasqually. Pasqually, a man enshrouded in enigma, established the Order of the Elus Cohens, or the Elect Priests, around the 1750s. This order was dedicated to theurgical practices aimed at restoring the original Adamic state of humanity, believed to have been lost due to the fall described in Judeo-Christian theology. Pasqually's system blended Christian mysticism with complex theosophical teachings, creating a unique pathway towards spiritual enlightenment and reintegration (McIntosh, 1997).

One of Pasqually's most influential disciples was Louis-Claude de Saint-Martin. Saint-Martin, often referred to as 'the Unknown Philosopher', diverged from the ceremonial practices of Pasqually and emphasized a more introspective approach to spiritual attainment. His philosophical writings, notably *Des Erreurs et de la Vérité* (*Of Errors and of Truth*) and *L'Homme de Désir* (*The Man of Desire*), underscored a profound contemplation of man's nature and his relationship with the divine. Saint-Martin's contributions significantly shaped the doctrinal evolution of Martinism, steering it towards a path that prioritized personal mystical experience over ritualistic theurgy (Waite, 2003).

Another key figure in the development of Martinism was Jean-Baptiste Willermoz. Willermoz played a crucial role in integrating Martinist ideas into Freemasonry, particularly within the Rectified Scottish Rite. This integration marked a significant moment in the history of esoteric and Masonic traditions, as it fused the mystical-philosophical tenets of Martinism with the structured, ritualistic framework of Masonic rites. Willermoz's work helped propagate Martinist thought beyond its original confines, allowing its principles to permeate a broader spectrum of esoteric practices (Mills, 2004).

This foundational triad of Pasqually, Saint-Martin, and Willermoz laid down the philosophical and practical bedrock of Martinism, each contributing unique perspectives and practices. Their collective influence established Martinism as a significant current within Western esotericism, characterized by its intricate blend of Christian mysticism, theosophical speculation, and ritualistic practice.

Martinism presents a unique confluence of Christian mysticism and theosophical elements. This integration, as analyzed by Antoine Faivre, reflects a distinct spiritual path that seeks to reconcile the mystic experiences of Christian tradition with the intricate metaphysical systems found in theosophy. Martinist thought often focuses on the inward journey of the soul, emphasizing personal experience and inner revelation. This path is seen as a means to attain a direct, experiential knowledge of God, transcending conventional religious practices and dogmas. The theosophical aspects bring in a more universalist approach, aiming to unveil the hidden dimensions of reality and the interconnectedness of all existence (Faivre, 1994).

Central to Martinism is the mystical concept of 'Reintegration', which diverges from traditional Christian teachings on original sin (Goodrick-Clarke, 2008). Instead, it emphasizes a process of returning to divine harmony through Christ, the Repairer, who is seen as the key to human spiritual restoration. This reintegration involves a reconciliation with God achieved through Jesus Christ's teachings, suffering, death, and resurrection, offering a path to restore the human condition. Unlike the conventional Christian emphasis on original sin, Martinism focuses on a transformative journey back to spiritual wholeness and harmony, reflecting its unique blend of esoteric beliefs and Christian mysticism (Goodrick-Clarke, 2008). This doctrine revolves around the fall of humanity from a primordial, divine state and the subsequent journey towards restoration and return. According to Martinist teachings, humanity's fall is not just a biblical or mythological event, but a spiritual reality that has distanced the human soul from its divine origin. The concept of reintegration, as expounded by René Guénon and others, is, therefore, the process of returning to this original state of divine unity, a journey that involves personal transformation, spiritual awakening, and moral rectitude. This concept is deeply rooted in Christian eschatology and has parallels in various mystical traditions (Roggemans, 2008).

The dualistic worldview in Martinism, as described by Tobias Churton, posits a clear distinction between the material and spiritual realms. Martinists perceive the material world as a realm of limitation, imperfection, and sometimes illusion, in contrast to the spiritual world, which is seen as the realm of absolute truth and divine reality. This dualism, however, is not absolute; the material world is not considered evil but rather a stage in the soul's journey towards spiritual perfection. The ultimate goal is not to reject the material world, but to transcend its limitations through spiritual knowledge and practice, thereby achieving a harmonious balance between the material and spiritual (Churton, 2005).

Theurgical practices in Martinism play a pivotal role, as Christopher McIntosh notes, in facilitating the practitioner's spiritual transformation and ascent. These practices, deeply embedded in the Martinist tradition, involve ritualistic actions intended to invoke divine energies or presences. The purpose of theurgy in Martinism is not merely to perform ceremonial rituals but to use these rituals as a means to achieve a higher state of consciousness and spiritual reintegration. These practices are seen as a form of spiritual alchemy, transforming the practitioner from within, aligning them more closely with the divine principle. The theurgical approach in Martinism is closely linked to the concept of 'operative prayer' or 'active meditation', where the ritual acts as a bridge between the human and the divine (McIntosh, 1997).

Martinist rituals and ceremonies, as described by Regardie, Cicero, & Cicero (2015), are rich in symbolic meanings and serve as a fundamental aspect of its practice. These rituals often incorporate elements from Christian liturgy, Masonic rites, and theosophical symbolism. They are designed to represent metaphysical truths and facilitate spiritual awakening. For instance, the use of specific symbols, gestures, and words in these rituals is not arbitrary, but is deeply imbued with esoteric meanings, reflecting the Martinist cosmology and the spiritual journey of reintegration. The rituals are typically conducted in a group setting within Martinist lodges, creating a shared spiritual experience that strengthens the bonds between practitioners, enhancing their collective journey toward spiritual enlightenment (Regardie et al., 2015).

Meditation and contemplation are crucial in Martinism, forming the core of its spiritual practice, as Arthur Edward Waite suggests. These practices are focused on inner silence, introspection, and the cultivation of a direct, personal experience of the divine. Unlike the theurgical practices, which are more outward and ceremonial, meditation in Martinism is about turning inward, exploring the depths of one's own being, and seeking communion with the higher self or the divine principle. This inward journey is considered essential for achieving the knowledge and understanding necessary for spiritual reintegration. It allows practitioners to transcend the limitations of the material world and experience a more profound, spiritual reality (Waite, 2003).

In examining the contemporary landscape of Martinism, it is evident that various Martinist orders have evolved, each preserving and adapting the tradition's teachings and practices to the modern era. As outlined by Mills (2004), these orders maintain the core principles of Martinism, such as the pursuit of spiritual reintegration, the practice of theurgy, and the study of esoteric Christian and theosophical doctrines. However, they may differ in their organizational structures, rituals, and interpretations of foundational texts. Modern Martinist orders often blend traditional teachings with contemporary spiritual insights, making Martinism relevant to present-day seekers. These orders function not only as custodians of the Martinist heritage but also as living communities that continue to explore and embody its mystical and philosophical teachings.

Martinism's influence on modern esoteric and spiritual movements is profound and multifaceted. Antoine Faivre (1994) highlights how Martinist thought has permeated various aspects of contemporary esotericism. Its emphasis on inner spiritual transformation, integration of theosophical ideas, and Christian mystical elements can be seen in many modern spiritual paths. Martinism has contributed significantly to the development of modern Western esotericism, influencing movements such as Theosophy, Rosicrucianism, and various forms of ceremonial magic. Its impact is also evident in the way contemporary spiritual seekers approach the integration of mysticism and ritual, as well as the quest for personal spiritual experience beyond the confines of orthodox religious structures. Martinism, with its rich heritage, continues to inspire and shape the evolving landscape of spiritual and esoteric practices in the modern world.

In an effort to promote the study of esotericism in France, Papus established a school initially known as the Groupe Indépendant d'Études Ésotériques (GIEE) in December 1889. The institution, located in Paris, later adopted the name Faculté Libre des Sciences Hermétiques in March 1897. Papus wrote to Sédir in 1901, acknowledging his founding role in establishing the École Libre des Sciences Hermétiques, saying, "You are a co-founder of our esteemed Hermetic School, and your teachings have profoundly influenced countless individuals. Whether in times of joy or during moments of strife, your unwavering commitment to your role has served as a guiding light for numerous souls who may have otherwise faltered and despaired" (Sédir, 1900, p. 1). Sédir was a close collaborator of Papus and played a significant role in the school's activities, which included editing and writing for the journal *Le Voile d'Isis*. Sédir also taught courses at the École Hermétique, including a series on Hebrew during the 1899-1900 session (Papus, 1913). Papus, again, in his own 1913 course taught at the Free Higher School of Hermetic Sciences, commended Sédir, saying he "has published an excellent work on Hebrew, a work of perfect erudition and very complete in its genre. Unfortunately, the edition was quickly sold out, and there are no more copies available today" (Papus, 1913, pp. 5-6).

This institution held a prominent position in the

field of esotericism, housing manuscripts from notable figures like Papus, Sédir, Jacques Barlet, Maurice Ourdeck, and Jeanne-Marie Poulat (also known as Geneviève Louis and G. L.). Among its courses, a noteworthy offering was a first-year Hebrew course in 1899-1900 taught by Sédir, which left a lasting influence on the study of esoteric knowledge and practices. Initially located within the offices of *Revue Spiritualiste*, a magazine founded by Papus, the school later relocated to its headquarters at 29 rue de Savoie in 1899.

The Free School of Hermetic Sciences drew a diverse and eclectic student body, encompassing artists, writers, and even politicians. Prominent individuals among its students and those influenced by its teachings, such as Aleister Crowley, Dion Fortune, and Rudolf Steiner, played substantial roles in carrying on the school's hidden and esoteric doctrines (Goodrick-Clarke, 2008, pp. 195-207). The prominent individuals among its students carried on, in a similar way to the view of Papus regarding apostolic succession, this hidden inner wisdom tradition, the absence of which would entail a collective loss in our limited perennial wisdom of the world and our place within it (Goodrick-Clarke, 2008, pp. 195-207). The curriculum covered an extensive range of subjects related to Western esotericism. The school's courses were taught by leading esotericists of the time, including Papus, Sédir, and Jules Doinel. Special courses and workshops, such as a series of Tarot lectures by Oswald Wirth (1900), complemented the regular curriculum.

The Free School of Hermetic Sciences significantly translated and published esoteric texts. For example, in 1898, the school published a French translation of the Kybalion, a foundational Hermetic text. Its influence on Western esotericism remains evident today, and it served as a model for establishing similar esoteric schools worldwide. École Libre des Sciences Hermétiques played a pivotal role in the resurgence of Hermeticism and the occult in Europe during the late 19th and early 20th centuries. Its influence extended to various esoteric movements and secret societies, such as the Hermetic Order of the Golden Dawn and the Thelemic movement founded by Aleister Crowley (Goodrick-Clarke, 2008, pp. 195-207). It continued operations there until its closure in 1939 due to World War II. Martinism's influence extended to other esoteric movements, including Theosophy and Anthroposophy (Goodrick-Clarke, 2008, pp. 195-207), marking its more implied yet profound impact on the landscape of new esoteric thought. In addition to their work on *Le Voile d'Isis* and the École Hermétique, Sédir and Papus collaborated on several other projects. For example, they co-authored a book on Kabbalah called *Kabalah: The Secret Doctrine of the Hebrews* (1903) (Sédir & Papus, 1903). They also worked together on translating Jakob Böhme's *Aurora* into French (Goodrick-Clarke, 2008, p. 196).

Papus' significant contributions to the study and practice of occult sciences left an indelible mark on the esoteric community. However, his life and career were tragically cut short by the ravages of tuberculosis, a disease Papus contracted during his involvement in the French Army medical corps during World War I. This unfortunate turn of affairs brought a premature end to his life and his influential career. Papus' death in 1916 marked the untimely end of a remarkable career in esotericism. His contributions to the study and practice of occult sciences, his founding of the GIEE and the Faculté Libre des Sciences Hermétiques, and his dedication to spreading esoteric knowledge left an indelible mark on the history of esotericism. His legacy continues to influence and inspire seekers of hidden wisdom to this day, but his absence was keenly felt in the esoteric circles of his time.

Sédir's teachings and theories were influenced by a number of spiritual, religious, and esoteric traditions, including Kabbalah, alchemy, Christianity, and Hinduism. He believed that all these traditions shared a common core of esoteric knowledge, which he sought to synthesize and present in a systematic way (Sédir, 1908, p. 10). He was directly influenced by the works of Emanuel Swedenborg, Jakob Böhme, Paracelsus, Heinrich Khunrath, John Dee, Johannes Valentinus Andreae, Robert Fludd, Tycho Brahe, Giovanni Pico della Mirandola, Johannes Trithemius, and Heinrich Cornelius Agrippa (Sédir, 1901, p. 5).

At the heart of Sédir's spiritual philosophy was the profound belief in the unity of all traditions. He perceived a common thread of spiritual wisdom that wove its way through Kabbalah, alchemy, Christianity, Hinduism, and beyond. Sédir's relentless conviction in this shared wisdom propelled him to embark on a mission of synthesis aimed at harmonizing and presenting these diverse teachings to the world. Central to Sédir's worldview was the concept of divine consciousness. He postulated that the entire universe was but a manifestation of this divine presence, a presence that permeated both the seen and unseen realms of existence (Sédir, 1898, p. 5). Sédir asserted that recognizing and forging a connection with this divine essence was paramount for spiritual growth and enlightenment, a belief that formed the very bedrock of his teachings (Sédir, 1899, p. 1).

Sédir held a firm belief in the potential for human advancement, championing the idea that individuals possessed the innate capacity to ascend to higher levels of consciousness. He viewed esotericism as a catalyst for awakening latent spiritual faculties and advancing along the path of self-realization. The concept of spiritual evolution stood as a cornerstone of his spiritual philosophy. He believed that human beings were on a continuous journey of growth and evolutionary development toward higher realms of consciousness. Life, according to Sédir, was a transformative process through which the soul evolved, with self-awareness and self-realization serving as pivotal milestones (Sédir, 1902, p. 10). Sédir also delved into the quest for the Divine Spark, referring to the inner 'Higher Self' within each individual. He considered the realization of this inner divine essence as central to personal enlightenment and fulfillment.

Practical esotericism was another pillar of Sédir's teachings. He stressed that theoretical knowledge alone was insufficient, advocating instead for direct engagement through meditation, prayer, and ritual (Sédir, 1902, p. 15). These practical exercises, he believed, could lead to transformative experiences and a deeper connection to the divine (Sédir, 1908, p. 15). Sédir had a deep appreciation for symbolism, recognizing its power to convey complex esoteric concepts in an accessible and evocative manner. He harnessed the potential of symbols extensively in his writings, considering them as gateways to deeper spiritual insights and understanding.

In his vision, Sédir placed great emphasis on the significance of community and fellowship. He held that individuals could derive immense benefits from being part of a supportive and spiritually oriented group. The exchange of ideas, shared experiences, and collective spiritual practices were viewed as invaluable elements of one's spiritual journey (Sédir, 1901, p. 20). Mystical experience was a recurring theme in Sédir's writings. His works delved into the nature of spiritual illumination, the inner voyage of the soul, and the transcendent facets of human existence. Sédir's goal was to guide individuals toward experiencing these mystical states firsthand. Nevertheless, Sédir's approach was not without controversy. His syncretism and eclecticism, as well as his willingness to draw wisdom from a wide array of sources and traditions, invited criticism from those who deemed his work overly eclectic and lacking in doctrinal consistency.

Symbols and mysticism continued to intrigue Sédir. He saw symbols as potent tools to access deeper layers of reality and to convey esoteric truths. Sédir's writings frequently explored the interpretation of symbols within various esoteric traditions. Drawing inspiration from alchemical symbolism, Sédir described the spiritual journey as an inner alchemical process. In this metaphor, individuals transformed their inner 'base' qualities into 'gold' or higher spiritual qualities, emphasizing the importance of inner purification and transmutation.

Meditation and contemplation featured prominently in Sédir's teachings. He underscored their significance as tools to access higher states of consciousness and connect with the spiritual dimensions of existence. Sédir firmly believed that regular meditation could lead to profound inner insights and spiritual experiences. Sédir's advocacy for brotherhood and unity underscored his belief that humanity should unite in mutual respect and cooperation, transcending cultural and societal divisions.

In an era marked by religious and sociocultural diversity, Paul Sédir stood as a champion for the unity of all religions—a concept that was still nascent during his time amidst evolving ideas regarding religious and societal relations. His religious syncretism, in many respects, mirrored the broader sociocultural changes taking place during the early 20th century.

It is a truism that a maelstrom of socio-cultural and religious transformations characterized the early 20th century. The advent of globalization, propelled by advancements in transportation and communication technologies, served to interconnect formerly disparate regions of the world, fostering an enhanced cultural exchange and economic interdependence. The process of industrialization led to significant urbanization, which, in turn, reshaped societal lifestyles and familial structures—this period also witnessed diverse religious shifts, with the ascendancy of secularism and the proliferation of novel spiritual practices.

In the broader sociocultural, political, and economic milieu of the early 20th century, this epoch was characterized by rapid transformations in the fundamental frameworks of social and political structuring. The shift from the established order to a novel paradigm represents an intrinsic dialectical advancement in the course of sociocultural evolution. Concurrent with Paul Sédir's era, as evidenced by the essence of his discourse, there emerged a notable trend toward enhanced interconnectivity among individuals and the hitherto discrete reservoirs of human knowledge entrenched within various religious, spiritual, and cultural paradigms that had previously existed in isolation. The advent of technological and scientific advancements has propelled human capabilities to new heights, enabling the consolidation of previously disparate reservoirs of knowledge into a unified collective understanding of the human condition. This shared intellectual treasury, encompassing the accumulated wisdom of humanity across time and space, was previously unattainable. However, it was within the historical context of Sédir's writing that the potential for such religious eclecticism and syncretism, as he advocated for, began to emerge. Sédir's syncretic

approach to spirituality was shaped by the broader
sociocultural context of his time, characterized by
a period of significant social transformation. The
increasing ease of travel, communication and the
emergence of mass media platforms facilitated the
dissemination of cultural practices on a global scale,
further propelling cultural exchange and blurring the
boundaries between traditional and novel ideas.

This period also marked a transition away from
the established social, cultural, and political order,
giving rise to revolutionary changes in religious,
sociocultural, political, and economic spheres. These
changes were driven by a questioning of traditional
norms and a yearning for new modes of organization,
thinking, and action. Amidst these cultural, political,
and social upheavals, Sédir's esoteric beliefs,
practices, and ideas emerged, reflecting the spirit of
innovation and the desire to transcend the limitations
of existing paradigms. Sédir's syncretism, therefore,
can be understood as a response to the dynamic
and transformative environment of his time. His
willingness to embrace diverse spiritual traditions and
integrate elements from various cultures reflected the
spirit of openness and the desire for a more inclusive
and holistic understanding of spirituality. In essence,
Sédir's syncretic approach was a product of his time,
a reflection of the broader sociocultural context that
emphasized the interconnectedness of cultures, the
questioning of traditional norms, and the pursuit
of new modes of thinking and action. Sédir's ideas,
though radical for his time, continue to resonate

with contemporary spiritual seekers who embrace a multifaceted approach to spirituality and seek to integrate diverse spiritual traditions into their personal belief systems.

In the pages of history, Paul Sédir emerges as a complex and enigmatic figure—a scholar, a teacher, and a mystic. While controversial to some, his eclectic approach has left an enduring legacy. Sédir's teachings continue to inspire seekers of esoteric knowledge, bridging the gap between the spiritual and the material realms. In an ever-evolving world, his work remains a timeless source of spiritual exploration, inviting individuals to unlock the mysteries of the universe and embark on their own transformative journeys.

References

Böhme, J. (1912). *Aurora: The Dawning of the Day in the Orient* [Aurora: Le lever du jour dans l'Orient] (J. Sparrow, Trans.). M. Watkins.

Churton, T. (2005). *Gnostic Philosophy: From Ancient Persia to Modern Times*. Inner Traditions.

Doinel, J. (1897). *Le Magnétisme humain: Étude théorique et pratique* [Human Magnetism: A Theoretical and Practical Study]. Chamuel.

Faivre, A. (2007). *Accès à l'ésotérisme occidental* [Access to Western Esotericism]. Gallimard.

Goodrick-Clarke, N. (2008). *The Western Esoteric Tradition: A Historical Introduction*. Oxford University Press.

McIntosh, C. (1997). *The Rose Cross and the Age of Reason: Eighteenth-Century Rosicrucianism in Central Europe and Its Relationship to the Enlightenment*. Brill.

Papus. (1913). *Premiers éléments de lecture de la langue hébraïque, par le Docteur Papus, G. Encausse. Les lettres, les nombres, les hiéroglyphes… Cours professé à l'École supérieure libre des sciences hermétiques* [First Elements of Reading Hebrew, by Doctor Papus, G. Encausse. The Letters, The Numbers, The Hieroglyphs… Course Taught at the Free Higher School of Hermetic Sciences]. Faculté des sciences hermétiques.

Papus, G. E. (1889). *Le Tarot des Bohémiens: Grand traité théorique et pratique de l'art divinatoire* [The Tarot of the Bohemians: A Comprehensive Theoretical and Practical Treatise on Divination Art]. Chamuel.

Papus, G. E. (1898). *Le Kybalion: Clef hermétique de la grande arcanologie* [The Kybalion: Hermetic Key to the Great Arcanology]. Chamuel.

Roggemans, M. (2008). *History of Martinism and the F.U.D.O.S.I.*. United Kingdom: Lulu.com.

Sédir, P. (1898). *La Voie mystique* [The Mystical Way]. Chacornac.

Sédir, P. (1899). *Le Royaume de Dieu* [The Kingdom of God]. Chacornac.

Sédir, P. (1900). *Éléments d'hébreu: Cours de première année professé à l'École libre des sciences hermétiques* [Elements of Hebrew: First Year Course Taught at the Free School of Hermetic Sciences] (Session 1899-1900). Avec une Lettre-Préface de Papus.

Sédir, P. (1901). *Les Sept Jardins mystiques* [The Seven Mystical Gardens]. Chacornac.

Sédir, P. (1902). *Les Plantes Magiques: Botanique Occulte, Constitution Secrète Des Végétaux, Vertus Des Simples* [Magic Plants: Occult Botany, Secret Constitution of Plants, Virtues of Simples]. Chacornac.

Sédir, P. (1903). *The Secret Doctrine of the Hebrews: Kabbalah* [La Doctrine Secrète des Hébreux : Kabbale] (A.E. Waite, Trans.). George Redway.

Sédir, P. (1908). *Manuel d'occultisme pratique* [Manual of Practical Occultism]. Chacornac.

Regardie, I., Cicero, C., & Cicero, S. T. (2015). *Gold: Israel Regardie's Lost Book of Alchemy*. Llewellyn Worldwide.

Waite, A.E. (2003). *The Mysteries of Magic: A Digest of the Writings of Eliphas* Lévi. Kessinger Publishing.

Wirth, O. (1902). *Le Tarot des imagiers du Moyen ge* [The Tarot of the Image Makers of the Middle Ages]. Chacornac.

DREAMS

Theory — Practice — Interpretation

In remembrance of Ant. C****,
The New (Dunamis) Power, Servant of Christ

CHAPTER I
DREAMS

The Mechanism of Dreams

Whether we look at the human being from the most diverse points of view, with the most profound and ingenious attention, the essential principle, and the central force by which we always see it moving, is *freedom*. This perfect essence has received many different names from theosophists. The Taoists and Boehme call it will; the Hindus, the supreme soul; the Gospel, a spiritual heart. Omnipotent in the kingdom of the Absolute, where one finds itself, as it passes into that of creation, at grips with two adversaries; or rather, it sees its movements circumscribed between two boundaries: *materiality and personality*. If it approaches the former, it organizes it and produces the bodies of all natures; if it approaches the second, it also organizes it, and, likewise, generates the spirits of all natures.

Let us now isolate an individual; we shall find in him a body, a spirit, a soul: the last being no more, in this mutable and temporary aggregate, than a secret flame, a witness, the invisible keystone of the whole edifice. The bodies and spirits will be the two obvious foci between which all the modes of personal existence will develop, just as the ellipse resulting from the circle enlarges or shrinks by the variations of the vector rays, while the primitive center of the mother-circumference occludes and abstracts itself.

Whether the bodily focus is exalted under the influence of a material stimulus (drugs, potion, perfume), a fluidic stimulus (animal magnetism), or an intellectual stimulus (occult science), it approaches the invisible world and enters it through the door below; physical life is suspended, psychic life no longer finds free cells to embody it, and the phenomena of presentiment, forecasting, and divination begin. The art which can provoke these manifestations is called magnetic somnambulism (e.g. sleepwalking).

On the contrary, if the spiritual focus goes out to meet the bodily focus, it imposes its stronger power on it, immobilizes it, and reduces it to temporary bondage. Then objects, scenes, creatures of the invisible world, the ordinary companions of the spirit, the forms of the environment which it usually inhabits, make their influence felt on the physical organism, take hold of it even as an instrument, and employ it for good or for evil in the execution of their desires. The Unreal opens through the door from above. This set of manifestations is called Thaumaturgy; they include dreaming, fury or enthusiasm, and rapture.

In the dream and the rapture, the consciousness of the physical becomes obnubilated, because of the weakness of the spiritual agent in the first case, because of its excess of strength in the second. As for enthusiasm, it constitutes the stasis of mystical equilibrium, where the individual keeps a full consciousness of wakefulness which is exercised simultaneously with the constant

and healthy collaboration of the god he has been able
to evoke.

Woe to that man if he has brought in an inferior
or even intermediate power! But if he has stretched
out his arms to God's arms, he knows eternal bliss from
this earth.

❄

We have just considered the genesis of the dream from
a principal point of view, in the world of the Empyrean
Heaven, as Heinrich Cornelius Agrippa (1486-1535),
would describe. Let us now look at a more naturalistic
aspect of the question.

The physical body, the assembly of chemical
molecules, is nothing if life does not bathe it. The
dream will, therefore, only be possible where matter is
animated. So the stone, the plant, and the animal can
have dreams.

As for man, if his celestial principle is not
provided with organs, he will remain in his place,
impassive, serene, and omniscient. There, the dream
does not occur.

For intelligence, it needs a starting point. It is not
the perception; it is what works on the perceived objects,
what gathers them, separates them, builds them,
expresses the juice of it, pursues the consequences of
it, and uses the indications of it. The dream is thus not
an intellectual activity, essentially.

But in us, the animal life and the intellectual life
are only two branches of a breath of life which is at the

same time movement, heat, light, mortal and immortal, mutable and fixed, centrifugal and centripetal. As it is the central animating force, it is held in the heart; from there, through the lung, it animates the blood, the vehicle of animal life; through the brain, it animates the mind, the vehicle of the intellectual life.

❧

Just as there can be living matter without thought, there can be thought without a body; there can be life without an organism. But this is only found in a metaphysics of abstractions, in those periods of biological neutrality, which Hindu occultism calls Layas (e.g. Laya Center) points. What is important for us is to understand that man today feels, knows, thinks, wants, perceives, imagines, and is passionate only by means of this vital center to which esoteric researchers have given so many names.

Many ancient theories could be reproduced here; but that one remembers the psychological quinary of the Kabbalists, that one analyzes the three souls of the Platonists, the seven principles of the hierophants of Thebes, the five envelopes of the Vedantins, the eight aggregates of the Buddhists, the seven forms of Boehme, the ternary of Swedenborg, the three symbols of alchemy, that one compares fifty other systems, from the Incas to Wronski, from the Druids to Kant, from the oceanic legends to M. Bergson, one fact remains, one conclusion is imposed. We will try to show this one and to make us understand.

❄

Man can perceive objects belonging to other modes of existence than the physical plane.

Experience shows this. But for the mind to be convinced of this, some insight is necessary. First, what is man made of? If you look through the old books you will find a hundred answers to this question, all of them more or less peculiar; but if you arrange them side by side, look for the concordances, and if you compare these concordances with the indications of simple common sense, you will find more or less this:

There is, in us, an absolute life and a relative life; the second is the garment of the first, its instrument, its school, its torment, and its glory. These two focuses go to meet each other, through cycles and universes; the ellipse tends to become a circle again. The first mode is the spark, the second is the wood; separated, they remain both lethargic; united, they feed each other and serve the life of the world. But, no more than we know the real nature of fire or of wood do we know our eternal self and our immortal self; we see games of them; and what we call the field of consciousness is the luminous zone formed in the atmosphere and on the floor of our body by the rays of the physical, animated, and intellectual creatures whose vibrations are related to those of our nervous ether.

All the rest of the world is only perceptible to us through dreams, raptures, prophetic delirium, and ecstasy, if it does not remain completely unknown to us.

In the center of man, in the Holy of Holies of

his inner temple, shines the eternal soul: impassive, unchanging, unmoved, omniscient, omnipotent, blessed. It is the window through which the other organs of the individual can see God; it attracts them unceasingly, it communicates its living force to them, it sublimates them.

Around this flame circulate the immense organisms of the human spirit, like an army of asteroids around its sun. And here we must understand each of our bodies, each of our fluids, our magnetic properties, our feelings, our mental faculties, and our powers of action as individual organisms, classified in hierarchical autonomy.

Each of these parts of ourselves is free, though drawn into the evolutionary line of the total self; in turn, this self is free, though it is driven physically by the planet, socially by the human race, and spiritually by religion. And so our physical body appears to be the medium through which earthly forms rise to the invisible and objects of the immaterial worlds fall to the visible.

❈

But, for perception to become conscious, it needs attention. This act is the first and simplest of the movements of the volitional sphere. The deeper, simpler, and more complete it is, the clearer, more truthful, and more fruitful the perception is. On the other hand, to perceive is to bring into contact a certain order of external vibrations with another order of nervous or sensory vibrations. If these two kinds of waves do not cross each other, for such or such a cause, there is neither contact nor perception.

Therefore, there must exist in the universe a certain number of imperceptible objects that are temporally imperceptible. Finally, attention is an inner movement transmitted through the mental, animistic, and/or magnetic ether, which forms the aura of the nervous force around the material body.

For perception to become conscious, there must be a second contact of the waves coming from the first spark indicated above with those of the centrifugal volitional current. So, among the perceptible objects of the Universe, only a small part enters our waking consciousness.

Now, if we could, by some artifice, modify the vibratory waves of our nerve cells, we would bring, by modifying at the same time the last stage of the attention process, a certain number of unknown objects into the field of our consciousness.

It is to obtain these modifications that all known psychic training tends: fasts, prayers, litanies, rosaries, mantrams, breathing exercises, excitants, magic mirrors, perfumes, religious ceremonies, and others.

However, Mother Nature offers us a very simple way to achieve the same result, without fatigue, without imbalance, without risk, without diet: it is sleep.

Physical man is a compound of several machines. When the steam engine runs out of coal, food supplies it; when the voltage in the electric machine weakens, sleep brings it back up.

The problem, then, is simply the wise use of the resources provided by Nature.

The nervous force in us is the product of the combination of the blood sent to the cerebellum with an imponderable matter: astral, if you will, which our fluidic body attracts and absorbs at the level of this same cerebellum. When the great sympathetic system uses all the available nervous force, the conscious nervous system, deprived of its means of action, stops, and sleep comes.

In this state, the body remains motionless and the senses inactive; psychic man is lightened of the material attractant, and he goes, in the hyper-physical spaces, to lead the life which is proper to him with more freedom than he could do during the wakefulness of the material body. For our spirit, or rather the different organisms of which it is composed, each has its own mode of existence, its habitat, its work, its days and nights.

When one of these psychic bodies makes an experience, meets an invisible, accomplishes a work – *since everything is held in us* - it can happen that the prolongation of its activity meets one of our nerves, one of our ganglions, a cell of our brain; the impression which results from this gives us, during the wakefulness, a sudden idea, an intuition, an apprehension or an alleviation; and, during the sleep, it produces a dream.

So that not all dreams are prophetic, the wheel of time may turn faster or slower in the world where our mind wanders than here on earth. We can see in dreams things that are past, things that are future, and even things that are present.

We will study the nature of these dreamed objects in the next chapter.

Another common cause of dreams is physiological disorders, especially those caused by congestion or anemia of the solar plexus.

Finally, one last cause, rare and unknown in its operation, is the intentional effort of an external will: *human, superhuman, or infrahuman.*

CHAPTER II
ᏩHE ᏗBJECTS OF THE ᏆREAM

In creation, the void does not exist. Its proper place is that abyss of Nothingness on which the billions of planets that make up the world navigate.

But, in the cosmic enclosure, everything is occupied. What the solid, the liquid, and the gaseous seem not to fill is penetrated by the fluidic. And the planes interpenetrate; the mother is separated from her son by a hundred leagues, but she is with him in the sentimental world; the artist toils and exhausts himself in front of his canvas, but his spirit cohabits with an angel of beauty in the aesthetic world; the philosopher pursues elusive concepts, but his intelligence converses with ideas in the metaphysical world.

Time nor space have absolute measure; they vary with the worlds. Everything is populated; the wood, the field, the road, the ruin, a wall, an empty room, a lake: teeming with invisible inhabitants whose number and activity would frighten us if we had our eyes and ears open.

In this portion of the earth's space that a stone occupies, corporeal spirits move, eat, sleep, think, and worship.

All stones are not flints; if the poor man cannot soften the miser, is it not that the feeling of compassion offers in him the hardness of a stone? A word here below can be elsewhere a flame, a hurricane, or a building.

Moreover, everything radiates. The mole does not pierce its galleries in a garden without, a few centuries later, some inhabitants of Sirius receiving the aftermath. The epigram that makes our guests laugh, do we know if it does not kill a being far away in the thicket of unknown worlds? And if, for our coffee, we choose the right sugar cube instead of the left one, have we counted how many creatures have been set in motion to achieve this tiny result?

Thus the horizon of intuitive conjectures is immense; the eye of the imagination, however penetrating, however quick, however daring, never manages to inspect it completely. Let us try, however, to count the races of creatures that populate the worlds; we will then have an idea of the objective causes of our dreams.

There is in Nature an immense current of evolution which tends to raise the light up to God, and an equally vast current of involution, by which God moves forward with pity, in the person of the Son, to meet His creature. In addition, the kingdom of Heaven has for twenty centuries been dispensing help and strength to every creature who asks for it. The inhabitants of each of these three universes can be perceived in the dream and give us something or ask us something. These three universes, their subdivisions into elements and planets, and their zodiacal specifications are the habitats of beings whose correspondence tables, demonology, angelology, and mythology of the different esoteric traditions draw up more or less complete lists.

Here is one of the broadest and most suggestive enumerations that can be found.[1]

In the world of evolution live seven kingdoms of creatures and in the world of involution also:

EVOLUTION	INVOLUTION	KINGDOM
The Number	The Laws	Citizens
The Mineral	The Spiritual Bodies	Families
The Energy	The Powers	Societies
The Planet	The Spirits	Divine Symbols
The Star	The Angels	Divine Choirs
The Animal	The Cherub	Servants of God
The Genius	The Archangels	Free Beings

Table I.

There are perfect affinities between each of the terms in these three lists. The groupings of matter call for laws; the effort of minerals calls for the spiritualization of bodies; energy brings power; vegetable life is analogous to spiritual life; the angels depend freely on one another, as the stars are linked to one another; the animal forms express materially the relations of the creature to the Creator which the cherubim express spiritually; finally the material being who has become free, the genie or the god, is the image

1 See Jacob, *Esquisse Hermétique du Tout Universel, 2nd edn* (Paris: Bibliothèque Chacornac, 1903).

of the archangel, a being who is one, living in God and
of God.

I. What appears as a number in ordinary
consciousness can be expressed as life, and expresses
an abstraction.
II. Ore comes from substance and produces flesh.
III. Energy comes from fluid and produces bodies.
IV. The plant comes from a spirit and produces
spirits.
V. The star comes from an essence and produces
angels.
VI. The animal comes from organs and produces
moral faculties.
VII. Genius comes from the sensory and is a product
of the intellectual faculties.

Similarly:

I. The laws are expressed in functions and in beings.
II. Spiritual bodies, into organisms and lives.
III. The powers, in properties and in movements.
IV. The spirits, in mental functions and in vegetative
functions.
V. The angels, in moral states and in biological states.
VI. The cherubim, in psychic states and faculties.
VII. Archangels, in pearls of wisdom and sciences.
VIII. The numbers can indicate any creature.

As for the mineral, in addition to the forms
that our science knows, it can be moral: such are our

virtues; it can be social: such are the bodies of collective entities.

Energy is the action of two balanced forces; the physical-chemical sciences study it; it is the invisible transition from mineral to vegetable.

The latter is a collective being obeying a spirit diffused in all its parts. Apart from the plants known to botany, a religion, a true secret society, a lineage, the force by which the body of the animal grows, these are plants.[2]

The kingdom of the stars has as its character a bond of reciprocity between all the constituent parts of a being. An egg, our viscera, an assembly of men fanatical about their leader, the woman of the Apocalypse, and a speaker are sidereal systems.

An animal is a collective being bound in its form and free in its movements. A people, beauty, intelligence, talent, the spiritual body, and the human race are animals.

Genius is a collective being, whose components are independent of each other but subject to a guiding will. The mythological gods, Adam, Manou, the Chinese Ren, a theater, a charitable society, and a family are genii.[3]

The individuals of each of these last six kingdoms are produced by the combination of the preceding kingdoms.

❈

---

2 Cf. the parables of the Gospels.

3 Cf. Jacob, *Esquisse Hermétique du Tout Universel* and *The Thousand and One Nights*.

The laws are the beings by which the existence of other subordinate creatures persists for a certain time; they are: mathematical, physical, organic, intellectual, moral, religious, and social. They govern wisdom, faith, feeling, thought, act, form, and ipseity. There is one for each kind of simple or collective creature.

The laws, combined between them, form bodies. Examples: associations, angelic armies, stock exchange operations, trade, a monastic order, a revolution, a fashion.

Power dominates the body and the law; it is always good, that is, in conformity with the divine will. Examples: gravity, the curve of civilization, Jesus, the anonymous good powers.

A spirit is essentially a collective with which all the cells have voluntarily associated themselves; it is a parasite that feeds on the being it haunts; it, therefore, goes where the environment is analogous to it; this is why vice or virtue grows in an automatic way. Crystal, fire, vegetation, generation, perfectibility, analysis, synthesis, and method are spiritual phenomena.

The angels are immaterial beings, individual, subject to many of their fellow creatures by means of a unique will. They provoke: they provoke our acts, our feelings, and our thoughts whether temporal or eternal. Their bodies are the families, the professions, the associations, and the species. They are immaterial stars. There are men who are angels and also angels who will never be men.

The cherubim are creatures of faith, of ideas.

The Scripture represents them in an animal form. They are the souls of all associations whose members are bound by a belief or an oath; they are nourished by faith, knowledge, power, imagination, intuition, inspiration, and ecstasy. They radiate from the being: from the faculties of sensation, perception, memory, instinct, and intellectual and spiritual discernment.

The archangel is a collective being made up of identical cells, united under a will whose wisdom constitutes its nourishment and environment. The archangel is sapient; he feeds on love; he is infinitely perfectible. Napoleon Bonaparte and his Guard were an image of the warrior archangel.

❧

The Kingdom of God also has its inhabitants, who appear in creation only exceptionally. The wicked and fanatics prevent them from living there; they are such by their work; they correspond to the numbers and laws.

They meet in families, which assemble like living crystals; they practice communism; there were some in Jerusalem immediately after the departure of Our Lord Jesus Christ. These are the prototypes of the spiritual bodies.

These families are grouped into corporations that feed on justice and carry out charity. The religions, in their beginning, are celestial societies; they are reflected in Nature as material energies and immaterial powers.

The combination of these three orders produces images, perfect and living symbols of one or more thoughts of the Father. He lets them be seen by certain men who describe them as best they can. Such are the divine ternary, the heavenly Jerusalem, the holy mountain, the throne of God; these signs are formed by divine mercy, and they radiate prayer. They become, in creation, spirits, and plants.

The material star and the immaterial angel are the figures of the divine choirs. The twenty-four apocalyptic elders are the true zodiac; the one hundred and forty-four thousand regenerated ones are also a choir. They praise God and thereby arouse true love in those who hear them, for their acts are harmonies. Pythagoras foresaw this when he spoke about the harmony of the spheres. These choirs are nourished by charity; that is why on this earth a musician of genius cannot but be good.

The servants of God are those souls in which faith lives with an omnipotent splendor; they are, therefore, the intermediaries between man and God, as the animals are servants of man and intermediaries between him and the cherubim. They possess what is true; they are the ones who can worship in spirit and in truth.

Men who have reached the peak of their perfection constitute the seventh divine kingdom, the Blessed. Of their freedom, of their ubiquity, the genii are an image; the archangels show us how powerful and pure they are. It is to them alone that belong the titles of Regenerate, Free Men, Children of Heaven; wherever they go, to accomplish the will of the Father, they are absolute masters.

❉

The description we have just read is the one most in keeping with the present reality of the world. One can undoubtedly choose another classification: stick to the fourteen Brahmanic Lokas, or to the twenty-five hierarchies of the Aankhyas, or to the nine choirs of the Kabbalists, or to the multiple Gnostic, scholastic or Hermetic phenomenologies.

But suppose one has been able to understand some of the endless lights that the Gospel brings. In that case, one will have felt at the same time, with an irrefutable certainty and depth, that everything is alive since "nothing that exists was made without the Word"; that all the immensity of the creaturely hierarchies can enter into relations with us; that there are only three great classes of beings: God's servants, God's enemies, and man; and that finally all that we perceive, all that we experience, all that we do is in the Light or in the Darkness, according to the present attitude of our heart.

Suppose someone knows how to realize in his intellect, in his feelings, in his fluidic forces, in his physical works, this unity that Christ has brought down with Him to this earth. In that case, he no longer needs analysis, science, or method to recognize himself in the labyrinth of worlds. The Master guides him every second and gives him truth and power whenever necessary.

Among all the visitors that the government of Providence sends to us unceasingly, there are some who are perceptible to our ordinary consciousness because they belong essentially to the same world as we do. We only become aware of the presence of other visitors in a fortuitous way, when one of our cerebral convolutions is purified enough to be able to enter for a few minutes with his mind into the apartments which are usually forbidden to us. This is the domain of intuition and dreams. But if man is not satisfied with these crumbs, he seeks ways to force these doors; these are called divinatory arts and magical training. But these methods are always illicit and eventually become harmful. This is what we will study in the next chapter.

CHAPTER III
ᎢHE ᎯᎡᎢ OF ᎠREAMING

O ur inner mind is constantly in touch with the invisible worlds; we do not realize this because the transmitting instrument is missing. We must, therefore, first make this registration easier and more extensive.

Here two methods meet:

The first is external. It recommends a series or series of graduated exercises which, based on a more or less true knowledge of the human machine, harmonize its functioning and subtly sensitize it. Everything depends here on the trainer's science. In manipulating such delicate and complex organisms, nothing is easier than making a mistake. The most serious and tenacious disorders can be caused by an error of diagnosis because of a badly chosen hour, a badly dosed stimulant, a false correspondence.

Do we know what a drug owes its virtue? Its use can bind our nervous body to unknown powers; we know the terrible consequences of morphine, cocaine, and alcoholic liquors. And all these substances do not bring a new force; their action is simply depolarizing: they take fluid from one point of the body to transport it to another, so that the unwise experimenter sees his general health become precarious and his will powerless to govern the irresistible impulses of his vegetative being.

The same criticism can be made of those puerile recipes which the superstitious populace uses: eating an apple with certain rites, writing barbarous names on ribbons; this seems harmless; but it is possible that an adventurous imagination or a weak will thus opens the door to unhealthy suggestions or manias.

As for the magic rite itself, whatever profit one proposes to make from it, the disadvantages are the same. Uncertainty about the quality of the result obtained, risks of illusions, probable fraud, violence exercised against certain invisibles, obligations unconsciously contracted towards other invisibles, disobedience to divine law, personal imbalance which can extend to physical illness: such are, in short, the pitfalls where the magician's fortune is often shattered.

Shall we turn to those more learned and more serene schools, where the student, after having conquered the mastery of his physical body, undertakes to control his fluidic body by respiratory observances, and his mental body by concentration? If he is successful in this kind of work, if the fruits he gathers seem nobler, healthier and more lasting, how much more murderous was their cultivation!

To restrict breathing is to increase the quantity of venous blood; it is therefore to stop the evolutionary march of a multitude of globules; it is to diminish the organic interchanges; it is to get out of the animal life a little.

To concentrate one's attention towards a constant *monoideism* is to build dykes against the floods of the association of ideas; but do we know if the mental image that we have chosen for exercise is not less necessary or less important than any of the others that are deliberately rejected?

On the other hand, these two unifications, that of the fluids and that of the ideas, cannot be achieved without a kind of vampirism exercised on the electro-telluric medium and on the mental medium, analogous to that by which an over-skilled financier knows how to attract money into his coffers. This is still taking what does not belong to us, and calls for an accounting in the future, without having given us, in the present, a healthy and complete certainty.

The prudent researcher will therefore reject all these more or less curious procedures, and will stick to a few rules of pure common sense, such as, for example, we will submit to the reader's examination.

We must prepare ourselves for a comforting night with a healthy and peaceful day. Worry spoils sleep; it is true that, at times, it cannot be completely controlled. To live healthily, one needs an ideal, and to live healthily, the highest of ideals is necessary. Just as the thrifty worker can nourish his body more hygienically, so he who lives according to an idea becomes an attractive center of forces, substances, feelings, and desires.

Now, an ideal is a living creature, whatever it is. It needs, like any creature, corporeal food, emotional food, intellectual food. The higher it is, the farther it is from this earth, the more effort it takes to evoke it.

It is therefore necessary first to conceive it purely, then to nourish it healthily, then to incarnate it with a serious, attentive, deep and permanent devotion. This is the most beautiful of the Great Works.

This happens quite naturally, for Nature is benign, as long as one forces oneself to be constant. One must not allow oneself anything — not an attitude, not a word, not a look, not an inner movement, not an impulse, not a stop — which is not in conformity with the goal one aims at. It is not useful to stay out of the common life; on the contrary, for the most imperative of our duties are in the family, in the profession, in the social function. It is these observances that keep us sane, that keep us in balance, and that advance our spirit most quickly.

This is the fundamental rule on which all the detailed prescriptions depend. Let us see how to adapt it to the goal we have in mind: to have true, clear, instructive, and remembered dreams.

The human heart lives in the plane where it wants to live. If it acts physically in greed, it will live in the spiritual realm of greed. If it is accustomed to lying, cunning, and concealment, the mind will become organically incapable of perceiving truth, any order of truths. In order to have true dreams, it is therefore necessary, by constant practice, to transform the tendencies of deceit and lies into acts in conformity with feelings, into feelings subject to the examination of the conscience, into thoughts which are the right deductions from feelings. We must get into the habit of not having any other secret will than the one we express by word and deed. We must keep our promises, we must know how to be discreet without being concealed. If, in this way, we make of our physical forces the workers of a heart that loves only the true, of our intellectual forces the forerunners of these healthy realizations, our whole being becomes an attractive magnet for the ideal to which we offer thus a cult of all the hours. And this ideal descends towards us through the interior spaces; it looks after us, comforts us, renovates our tirednesses, and recreates, so to speak, all our energies, until those of the body of flesh. Then everything in us becomes true; error flees from us; and, not deceiving the confidence of any visible creature, no invisible one has the power to deceive ours. Our dreams become true.

❀

The clarity of our dreams depends on material and spiritual physiological conditions.

It is necessary that the invisible agent has sufficient nervous force. Therefore, take only light, easily digestible food at the evening meal: no stimulants; go to bed as early as possible, so that the physical rest, almost complete at midnight, leaves the brain free around one or two o'clock in the morning.

It is always healthier to get up very early than to stay up late.

It is better to place the bed with the head to the north or east. The color of the drapes and fabrics in the bedroom is important. White is healthy, but dispersive; red is too exciting; brown is heavy. It is better to choose, according to personal taste, shades of gray, yellow or blue. Walnut wood is not very recommendable, nor is oak; if you want a metallic bed, choose copper.

Light should not be kept on during sleep, or, if it cannot be dispensed with, it should be in a purple or mauve night light, or behind a curtain, so that the rays do not fall on the sleeper's head.

To be absolutely safe, one should not sleep with the window open, provided that the room is very ventilated during the day. If you can't sleep in an enclosed space, draw a curtain in front of the window.

Keep metal objects in the room as little as possible. If the spouses make their bed together, it is better that they do not change places in order to keep the direction of the magnetic interchanges.

If the nights are restless, use the smell of wood or juniper berries, to the exclusion of all other perfumes.

Here are some psychic precautions.

Let the mind be lucid during the waking hours;

it will be so during the dream. It is therefore a question of fully possessing what is called presence of mind. And, for that, to practice in the following way:

1° Think of only one thing at a time. This is a long process; it requires calmness and patience; understand that true strength is quiet and not agitated; slowly bring your attention back to the work in progress; take time, you will regain it later;

2° Practice changing work faster and faster; to grasp at a glance a great variety of objects, the details of a costume, of a display, the particularities of a street; learn to see, to observe, with precision;

3° Train yourself to keep your composure in front of a fortuitous case or an accident; to have the right gesture and the right answer always ready.

The habit thus acquired of fully possessing oneself will confer on the will a power of control that it will no longer abdicate even in sleep, which will allow us not to be passive machines, to be able to move in a dream, to make decisions, to speak, to act. A whole unknown world will open up before us, a vast field of captivating possibilities, energies that were previously embryonic will develop within us; Nature will take on a new meaning, and our total being will be modified, clarified, and energized.

❄

We saw in the previous chapter what the sources of our dreams are. In fact, as we have already explained, we only see in sleep the pictures of the country that inhabits the inner man. It is, consequently, the predilections of this one that we must improve; it is to the personal help that the living Providence sends us by the ministry of its visible and invisible agents that we must make him attentive.

For the law of attractions which governs the physical order also governs the hyper-physical order. Our desires, which we try to realize in matter, the inner man also pursues in the Invisible. The prevailing passion seeks satisfaction with as much ardor in sleep as in wakefulness.

Consequently, it is important to take the following precautions:

1° Before going to bed, catch your breath, so to speak; a clear and concise recapitulation of the day will establish progress or setback. As for the night that is beginning, the Sunday prayer includes all the thanks and all the useful requests, because our material bread is assured since we work; it is the bread of the soul that it is urgent to inquire about. During the day, it is effort, trial, and suffering that provide it; in sleep, it is dreams;

2° It is necessary, therefore, for a few minutes, to forget one's troubles, to forget one's sufferings, to enter with a deep and simple desire into the love of God and into the spirit of the ever-present Master; to ask Him for the Light and the means of understanding it, for the favor of remembering it and for the strength to spread it; for, I repeat, the dream can instruct us and can also make us do someone a favor;

3° To keep oneself in the greatest possible abandonment of oneself and of all that relates to oneself, in order to leave the door open to the unforeseen from Above, to the human impossible, to the divine possible;

4° Finally, if one has promised to pray for a sick person or for a friend in pain, one must do so despite one's own fatigue. When, moreover, the day's work has been too arduous, the Father does not require long prayers: an impulse of the heart is enough, although it is better to say it aloud.

❧

To remember dreams, the precautions previously described will be of great help.

The purer our heart, the more ardent our desire for the Light, the more our inner self trusts in God, the more vivid will be the nightly impressions.

Nevertheless, it is good to have a pencil and paper with you when you start this school; it is possible, with a little energy, to wake up for a few seconds to write down the dream you have just had. In any case, it is necessary, with the awakening, to make an effort of calm and quiet memory, in order to write a record that one will preserve.

We must mention everything, even the seemingly insignificant details, even the most vague memories; one word can reconstruct a whole scene; there are sometimes dreams with two or three planes which are entangled, split up, and come together in turn.

It is therefore a good idea to set aside, as soon as one's eyes are open, a few minutes of calm recollection during which, if the brain is accustomed to it, the memories will come back, vivid and precise.

CHAPTER IV

⌒HE ⌒NTERPRE⅂A⅂ION OF ⅁REAMS

The importance and truthfulness of the dream depend, as do the importance and truthfulness of all the manifestations of our life, on the depth of the invisible plane which our spirit inhabits.

There are, therefore, two great qualitative classes of dreams: those which belong to any one of the innumerable planes of Nature; and those which come from that central plane, the heart and pillar of the world, where divine solicitude shines forth with constant brilliance, in the form of the Friend who is the Alpha and Omega of all the universes.

Those who have not devoted themselves body and soul to the service of God will have dreams of the first class, the symbolism of which will depend on their dominant preoccupation, their temperament, their unimaterial genealogy.

In the tradition of the Hermetic sciences there are many methods of interpreting oneirological images. All peoples have data on this art; but only Arab, Israelite, and native documents have come down to us.

The Arabs have left many books of oneiromancy, although all empirical, without system, without key. However, they had a secret method of interpretation, based on astrology, which the Rosicrucians of Egypt had taught them, and whose traces can be recognized in the work of Jean Belot, parish priest of Milmonts.

However, the divinatory procedures require, to provide some certainty, a very long practice and a subtle intuition. Moreover, they are artificial methods which only bring us into contact with the external reality of the invisible in a mediated way.

It is preferable, from all points of view, to study the dream directly by appealing only to the intimate sense, by listening to life speaking to us, by looking with a clear eye at the nocturnal pictures where our imagination moves.

Let's note some general points.

First, there is no universal key to dreams. A scene will have a different meaning for you than for the person next to you, because your mind is not in the same place as his. However, it may be that the members of a close-knit family, or of a contemplative community perfectly submissive to its angel, have dreams whose key is the same for all. But, in the present state of our development, these are very rare cases.

Secondly, it is necessary to distinguish whether the dream is a recollection of the past or a premonition. If the characters that appear in it have only heads and no bodies, it is almost always a scene from a previous existence. The other dreams are generally of the future. The closer they are to morning, the closer their realization, because the sleeper's mind sinks in the evening from the outside to the inside of the world, and returns after midnight from the inside to the outside. This is why some ancient schools of wisdom gave special importance to nightly prayers and contemplations.

Imagine a planet that moves ten thousand times slower than the Earth. For its inhabitants, one of its nights will last ten thousand of our terrestrial nights; their sleep will thus have dreams ten thousand times more extensive than those of an Earthling. Their spirit will be able, while dreaming, to live a life here below, from birth to death. This is to show that, in dreams, everything is objectively real.

Third, the day of the week influences the dream, and the planetary hours in each night.

The Sun influences the dream from midnight on Saturday to midnight on Sunday, and so do the other heavenly bodies.

As for the hours, here is a table:

Sunday from Midnight to Noon:

From Midnight to 1 a.m.	*The Sun*
From 1 a.m. to 2 a.m.	*Venus*
From 2 a.m. to 3 a.m.	*Mercury*
From 3 a.m. to 4 a.m.	*The Moon*
From 4 a.m. to 5 a.m.	*Saturn*
From 5 a.m. to 6 a.m.	*Jupiter*
From 6 a.m. to 7 a.m.	*Mars*
From 7 a.m. to 8 a.m.	*The Sun*
From 8 a.m. to 9 a.m.	*Mars*
From 9 a.m. to 10 a.m.	*Mercury*
From 10 a.m. to 11 a.m.	*The Moon*
From 11 a.m. to Noon	*Uranus*

Sunday from Noon until Midnight:

From Noon to 1 p.m.	*Jupiter*
From 1 p.m. to 2 p.m.	*Mars*
From 2 p.m. to 3 p.m.	*The Sun*
From 3 p.m. to 4 p.m.	*Venus*
From 4 p.m. to 5 p.m.	*Mercury*
From 5 p.m. to 6 p.m.	*The Moon*
From 6 p.m. to 7 p.m.	*Saturn*
From 7 p.m. to 8 p.m.	*Uranus*
From 8 p.m. to 9 p.m.	*Mars*
From 9 p.m. to 10 p.m.	*The Sun*
From 10 p.m. to 11 p.m.	*Venus*
From 11 p.m. to Midnight	*Mercury*

On Monday, from midnight to 1 a.m. the action of the Moon takes place, and so on until the end of the planetary series.

In modern treatises on astrology, a series of correspondences can be found in order to situate the dream under one of the seven astral categories.

The influences of the lunation and those of the other planets are not active enough to be taken into account.

Fourthly, we will distinguish the symbolic dream from the pure and simple forecast according to whether the scene will or will not be illuminated by the sunlight.

Fifthly, when the dream relates to personal events in our moral life, its omen will be either good or bad in the opposite direction to the joyful or sad character of the dream scene.

Sixthly, natural dreams assume the ordinary symbolism by which their plan usually manifests itself to the human intellect. An alchemist will see patterns, numbers, and signatures. One who has no special purpose in life will dream in the forms of ordinary objects and ordinary individuals. A mathematician, however, will not dream of the true forms of numbers; their planet is too far from ours; just as an intellectual philosopher will not be able to perceive, for the same reason, the genius of the ideas which preoccupy him.

Finally, the great secret to put oneself in communication with this immense invisible ocean where all the terrestrial creatures, all the physical events, all our states of consciousness exist a priori, is not to study, nor to analyze, nor to discuss; it is to want or, rather, it is to love. If we truly love, that is to say if we know how to put ourselves in the place of our neighbor, of the animal, of the plant, of the stone, in order to carry a little of their burden, these beings come to us and in us; they are the ones who are the most important.

They open the doors of the imagination, they teach it their language, and we understand their requests and their warnings.

❄

But this is difficult; and the few men who have the courage to take this path already belong to the small cohort of the soldiers of Heaven. For them the whole universe takes on a new aspect and a more intimate meaning. Instead, for example, of seeing in a dream the refraction in this or that plane of the essential form of a creature, they are brought into the presence of that form itself. They know the spirit of things; they have crossed the region of hierarchies, correspondences, classes and kinds; they have reached beyond the elements, further than the planets, higher than the fixed stars.

Since they are devoid of egoism, without greed, harmless, the invisible creatures visit them with confidence, as the animals of the forest come around the immobile gymnosophist. And they can talk to these creatures, and act on them. Their sleep is not inaction, although it rests the physical body.

Seeing therefore, several nights, several months, several years even in advance the picture of an event, an illness, a catastrophe, such men understand at once the meaning of the vision, and they control themselves enough to be able to intervene after having asked their Master for the license. They can modify such and such a picture, drive away such and such a harmful animal, rescue such and such a creature.

Often the Master takes them with Him, either on His winged horse or on His ship; He makes them visit unknown regions, strange races; sometimes they go to battle; it is a great reward for them to be able to give to the Light something of their own strength and their own heart.

CHAPTER V
ⱢEXICON OF ⰄREAMS

W

e want to give here only a few interpretative examples of the dreams which we have just discussed and which can be described as divine. No formula for personal action was indicated during dreams of this kind, because of the great importance of leaving each disciple complete freedom, or rather, because of the respect that must be paid to the Master by submitting in advance to the conduct that he will see fit to hold towards His pupils. Such psychology is as personal as the interpretation of the dream itself. All things are possible to God; His action is not contained by any framework; no human intelligence can embrace it; and it is the inner realization of these concepts that gives us that spiritual poverty without which the kingdom of God remains closed to us.

The following meanings are, therefore, only accurate for the one who carries out more or less the work indicated by the Gospel.

❋

There are two opposite desires in man: that of the earthly man and that of the spiritual man. The first wants to conquer everything: matter, money, glory, science, and power. The second is only concerned with the conquest of Heaven.

It is the former which exerts the dominant influence on our present consciousness, and it is by this influence that we appreciate as happiness or misfortune the events which occur. But the interests of the spiritual man are opposite. What is a cause of joy to him is a sorrow to the earthly self. And vice versa.

So the servant of Christ will interpret the images of the dream in the opposite way to what they would mean in the current mentality; for it is his spiritual self that acts in sleep; his joys thus presage sorrows for the earthly self, his elevations of its abasements, his sorrows of material successes for the earthly self.

By combining these data with the general symbolisms of the march, of the struggle, of natural phenomena, interpreted in the sense of the Spirit, one will be able to obtain indications quite easily.

Besides, if one observes one's dreams, it would be credulous to attach to each of them an important meaning. We generally live too much in moral error for spiritual truth to be perceived with accuracy by us. This is why oneiromancy is a very approximate science.

❧

General Symbolisms of Dreams and Their Meaning:

Slaughterhouse. — Filled with livestock: material wealth.

Abbot, abbess, monk, nun. — Test: physical, moral or intellectual; initiation; school, discipline. Religious orders and ecclesiastical states each have a precise meaning according to the asceticism of the dreamer.

Bees. — Wealth; observe if they are killed, if they are collected, or if they attack

Abyss. — Danger to run, even from health.

Childbirth. — Happiness or wealth, if it is easy.

Eagle. — Extraordinary things.

Needle. — Pertaining to love.

Garlic. — Pertaining to mysterious things.

Wings. — To have: great spiritual elevation.

Food. — Good or bad omens according to their flavor. Reversal of the omen to the spiritual.

Larks. — Joy or wealth.

Love. — If one is happy in a dream, it is a danger to the physical.

Donkey. — In good condition, loaded: success of efforts.

Animals in a herd. — Abundance: of money, if they are sheep; of children, if they are lambs; of goods, if they are oxen; of news, if they are horses. The color of the animals indicates the quality of what they portend.

Trees. — Good or bad, depending on whether they are deciduous or not.

Weapons. — Honors.

Automobile. — Advancing completely and freely, internally.

Ostrich. — Profit, travel, rich and beautiful women.

Amphibian. — Serious illness, ulcer, cancer, etc.

Ram. — Great character.

Shepherd. — Marriage, spiritual foundation.

Injury received. — Success.

Oxen. — Abundance if they are in good condition

Bouquet. — Punishment.

Scholarship. — Secret.

Bullfinch. — Joy.

Arm. — Power, reception; or mourning if it is cut off, etc...

Slander. — Discovery of our faults.

Burglar. — Madness for those who receive their visit.

Camp. — Honor, bravery.

Duck. — Property derived from a woman.

Cellar, cave. — Bad companies or enterprises.

Field. — Fruitful work to be undertaken.

Hunting. — Success according to the kind of animal that is killed.

Cat. — Deception of friends.

Shoe. — Woman.

Path. — Easy, difficult, or processive, depending on whether it is straight, level, or steep.

Railroad. — Advancement more than our merits allow.

Horse. — News.

Hair. — A sign of greater or lesser spiritual power according to its dark or light color and its greater or lesser length. Its fall means illness.

Dog. — Friend.

Cabbage. — Ideas will come.

Fall. — Disgrace, failure. Be careful and loyal. College, boarding school.- Trial, discipline, boredom.

Hill. — Celebrity.

Fight. — Good; especially if you see blood flowing.

Rope. — Help, link, depending on the attachment of the rope.

Color. — Whether for plants, animals, clothing, or human beings, indicates spirituality and goodness the closer it is to white.

Crocodiles. — Police, policemen.

Teeth. — If they fall out, death of parents; if they grow, birth of children.

Devil. — An enemy.

Water. — Good, bad or dangerous signs, according to its clarity or rapidity.

Crayfish. — Discussion, disappointment.

Squirrel. — Friendship.

Church, religious building. — Trial, all the more so if the service is celebrated there, if you sing there, and if the officiants take care of you.

Ink. — Prosperity.

Enemy, animal or man who attacks. — Disease.

Sword. — Child. Marital affairs.

Hermit. — Beware of loneliness.

Stars. — Hope or not, depending on their brightness. If they fall, disaster. They also represent science, fame.

Excrement. — Justified rumors.

Flour. — Prosperity.

Woman. — Good or bad, according to her color, from blonde to red.

Woman with a fiery face. — Fever.

Farm. — Ease; good spiritual work.

Flowers. — Suffering, tears.

River, etc. — If it is clear, peace, success.

Hay. — Comfort.

Lightning. — Fruitful success; great news.

Fruit. — Out of season: good material sign. Love.

Constable. — Upcoming punishment.

Knee. — Relates to material work

Clothing. — The less you show yourself dressed, the more people will know you; to see someone naked is that we will be informed about his true character. As a result, more or less severe humiliation for the person we see is more or less undressed.

Grass. — Good sign.

Swallows. — The more numerous they are and the more they fly, the better the news will be.

Small and sinister man. — In a vineyard, phylloxera.

Clock. — The existence of the dreamer in general.

Flood. — Bad for your health.

Insects. — Enemies.

Justice. — Trial.

Plowman, peasant, farmer. — Good sign: healthy, spiritual activity.

Lake. — Wealth, peace, friendships.

Lion. — Excellent, spiritual protection, especially if one converses with him.

Bed. — Represents the fiancée, the wife.

Wrestler. — He is a force of nature; be careful.

Active hand. — Powers.

Public house and everything related to it. — Gains, financial operations, more or less happiness according to the actions of the inhabitants of these places.

Death. — Internal processing. See dead, upcoming deaths in the family.

Flies, insects, spiders. — Hassles, annoyances, domestic pitfalls.

Moustache. — Goods.

Ship, etc. — Change good or bad depending on the circumstances.

Navel. — The wife.

Ocean. — The people.

Goose. — Profits.

Birds. — News.

Omnibus. — Money essential on a day-to-day basis.

Bear. — Building with manual-laboring tenants. Enemy.

Straw. — Material goods.

Umbrella. — Preservation.

Parents. — News.

Impoverishment — The people.

Comb. — Material improvement.

Pelican. — Sacrifice to be made, where one will be a priest and a victim.

Stones. — Bad signs.

Octopus. — Taxes, owners, financial administrations.

Pipe. — Meditation.

Public square. — Complications clarified.

Plants. — Flowers mean pain; plums mean falsehoods, deceptions; nettles mean attacks, vexations; wild gourds mean tranquility; the meadows mean feasts of the Church; cherry means ingratitude, adultery, betrayal;

walnut means fighting, persecution.

Rain. — Blessing, fertilization — troubles, but having good results.

Chest. — Moral qualities.

Lungs. — Women or servants.

Prayers. — Long test, especially if you sing or play a musical instrument.

Dew. — Blessing.

Blood. — Success according to the scene in which it flows.

Wild boar. — Dangerous, run away from it.

Snakes. — Illness, fever, choking.

Thirst. — Concerns; torments; worries.

Soldiers. — Good; all the better because they belong to a more special weapon; only work and responsibility. If one wears the uniform, it is a sign of spiritual power.

Sun. — Excellent omen.

Sovereign. — Success or failure according to their good or bad reception.

Skeleton. — Death.

Carpet. — Represents the existence of the dreamer.

Bulls. — Flee from them because they signify punishment.

Storm. — Inevitable danger.

War. Land, Terrain. — The state of fortune.

Theater and what is related to it. — Deceit, falsehoods.

Pest/Vermin. — Destitution, holiness, sanctity.

Worms. — Diseases, angina, neuralgia, troubles.

Old age. — Good solution for trouble.

Virgin Mary. — Certain protection.

Flying in the air. — Vanity. Travel.
To vomit. — Displeasure, public affront.
Eyes. — Feeling; things of the heart.
Zodiacs. — One will receive new ideas on Esotericism, in theory or in practice.

The nations appear in their heraldic forms. China is represented by a dragon, Russia by a polar bear, India by an elephant, and England by her leopard.

Religions are represented by their usual emblem. The sciences and the arts, by their common emblems; the trades and the professions are very easily recognizable. The saints sometimes appear, or rather the churches dedicated to them. Thus the church Saint-Augustin means, for a Parisian, trouble with women; the church of Saint-Laurent, material trouble; Notre-Dame, intellectual trouble. If the canonized saint shows up, he means according to the role that popular belief attributes to him, as a healer, a helper, etc. The popular instinct is almost always true.

Finally, let us remember that any of the dreams in our second category has a personal meaning, a social meaning, a political meaning, a religious meaning, a cosmic meaning, a mystical meaning, and a psychic meaning; and that the elaboration of this dictionary, which is the true individual key to the dreams, requires a daily and continuous work, which a single existence is not enough to perfect.

The sooner we begin it, the sooner we will be able to draw precious lessons from sleep.

Magic Letters

PREFACE TO THE ORIGINAL EDITION

MY DEAR SÉDIR,

According to your Custom, you still open a new way to the adaptations of the occult. So far, our indigestible and technical treatises have put off many readers. It was necessary to give to the aridity of mystical subjects the literary adaptation that no one, better than you, was capable of realizing.

You have tried, and at the first attempt, you have succeeded beyond all hope in the following pages.

If you will bring back the *ideal* to a few more souls, you know that your reward will be great enough to make it unnecessary for me to overwhelm you with more praise. He who has done his duty has well-deserved heaven and I have always been happy to find in your friendship support in the struggles and assistance in the common effort. It only remains for us to wish you a second and even more enlarged edition of these "seducing magic letters" which are appearing today. In the meantime, always believe I am your old comrade.

Gérard Encausse i.e. Papus, (1865 - 1916).

PROLOGUE

My friend Désidérius, who died many years ago, was a very bizarre character, if one designates by that word the originality of an implacable logic that consults only itself to conduct itself in the Universe. He was born poor, but his application was precocious, and his business intelligence allowed him to quickly repair this oversight this oversight of fortune! As I saw in college, upsetting the pedagogical routine, in the same way he continued in life to cut the quincunxes and ransack the flowerbeds of this beautiful park that is the modern bourgeoisie. Being bored by craftiness as much as by formality, he always proceeded with a childlike aspect, and people did not see the acuity of his gaze, but everyone exclaimed: How lucky is he!

Other worries for commercial sympathies and neighboring curiosities: to what were the respectable profits of the Désidérius house put? Skilled surveillance was organized to discover which of his friends' wives he preferred; cheerful brewery companions, whose curiosity inspired trapper's tricks, followed him on rainy evenings to the music halls or on the mornings of his frequent runs in the suburbs: Nothing, not the slightest dust cloud on the horizon, not the slightest soubrette in his home, not even a hint of those aesthetic vices by whose names Germany, France, and England refer to each other.

Serendipity served the curiosity of our investigators well when, one of them leading his family to the pond at Luxembourg Gardens, like a mother hen with her chicks, saw at the corner of the Pont-Neuf Désidérius, his arms loaded with old books, his bulk over the cases of the booksellers; the key to the enigma was found; our man had to be some researcher of strange chimeras, maniac collector, or whimsical scholar.

Without wearying the patience of the willing reader any longer, I will reveal to them that Désidérius collected ancient books. What were they? I have never been able to know. When did he read them? Mystery! For what purpose? Impenetrable as the providential will.

The fortunes of noctambulism brought us together; the first word he spoke to me was to rectify an error of diagnosis that I had just made deciphering hypothetical hieroglyphs in the soft hand of a girl; he knew how to pique my curiosity at the first word; his system of palmistry was neither that of Desbarroles nor that of D'Arpentigny, and did not agree with the lessons of any of the old masters of the sixteenth. He had a way of reading in hand, looking down on it, which reminded me of that of the Gypsies of England, and I knew later that his system was that of the Hindu Tantras.

One curious about rare things, such as I, could not but be drawn to this unexplored track; but Désidérius, very cleverly, did not let himself be taken in by the diplomacy of my conversations; he always brought them back towards the monotonous ground of business, the banal life and the vulgar topics from which his singular perspicacity made spring unexpected comparisons and instructive analogies. This was indeed the character of his mind: he seemed to possess a novel cerebral circumvolution that penetrated the depths of being: a magnifying glass that, disregarding differences, allowed only the similarities of the most diverse objects to appear to the observer from the outside.

He had to know the law of things and to know how to group them according to their inner genesis; one would have said that he was similar to a traveler resting on the top of a mountain and taking from above a clear and real view of the country of which, lost in the valley, he had only glimpsed some aspects without cohesion This solitary spectator of life resembled a lord: tall, lean, with a shaven face, brown skin, and chestnut hair, always dressed in fabrics of uncertain colors; he looked as if he had come down from a Rembrandt frame. He seemed drowsy; he spoke quietly, laughed little, and under his splenetic air hid an extraordinary stamina to physical fatigue such as from office work. I never saw in Désidérius the sign of any passion: in the face of awkwardness or ill will, his voice became more caressing and his forehead more serene: but the obstacle always disappeared quickly by a chance circumstance; then he made it the text of a small lesson of the psychology of the people or even of the things, because it was one of his favorite theories that the events live, that they have their anatomy, their physiology, and their biology, and that one can govern them as one arrives at the end of an indocile and capricious child.

Around this time, I became enamored of historical and archaeological studies, and I focused my research on the mysterious brotherhood of the Templars. All historians agree that this order was a society of clever, ambitious, and greedy businessmen; I was soon convinced of the falsity of this opinion. Thanks to old friendships, I had free access to the private libraries of certain scholars in Germany and England; and it was there that happy discoveries gave me the pride of astonishing the learned world with an original and new thesis. I was able to reconstitute their rites, to unveil that it was the too-famous Baphomet that had degenerated into a little lapdog in the 18th century, to make known the works carried out in the commanderies and the reason for the imposing architectures of these primitive masons.

One evening, I was telling Désidérius about my work, thinking that I would surprise him and be ready to compliment him when he answered one of my questions: "It is very good to have worked on this question: your idea is ingenious, but you will never exhaust it entirely because you lack the metaphysical thesis of your physical antithesis."

I did not understand, and I asked, "A metaphysical thesis?"

"Yes, if the earth exists, it is because there are two, and if the heavens rise above our heads, it is because the earth is under our feet," explained Désidérius with a half-smile. "I am giving you formulas that are too general; you are not yet accustomed to grasping at once the radiations of an idea; it is, however, a necessary thing.

Thus, for the matter at hand, you have not made the simple observation that if the Templars have given rise to a legend, that legend is their reflected ghost, their analogical opposite. If you believe them to be an association of money-changers and bankers, it is because their real wealth came from a completely different source; if you know vaguely what they did in the upper rooms of their fortresses, it is because you are completely unaware of the use of their cellars and underground galleries where the real life of the Order circulated, active and elusive.

This is what you could have seen."

"Your idea is original, to say the least," I replied, "but on what precise documents do you support it? Do you have any proof?"

"My dear friend," replied Désidérius, taking equal puffs from his pipe, "every intellectual notion has as much and more reality than this marble table or this coffee cup, but there are many things that people do not need to know; our eyes are conformed to receive such a quantity of luminous energy, but you know very well that too much brightness blinds us. Everything in the universe is perfect."

"What about these documents?"

"Oh, we'll see later; you must first get rid of a certain mental background which, instead of helping you, creates a wall. If you want to live, start by killing the old monster inside you."

"Come on, now you're going to give me mysticism. I have read Jacob Boehme, the cobbler ..."

"But you didn't apprehend him?"

"Did you?"

"Oh me! One has to give oneself an interest in life."

"But will I ever see your documents? I am sure you must have treasures, so why don't you let me see a little of them? You know that I know Lord L***, who has such a beautiful manor house and druidic antiquities in the Highlands. I have entered the library of Mr. S***, who has spent his life collecting Tibetan manuscripts, and the triply sealed one of Professor K*** of Nuremberg, where all Western mysticism is to be found, along with the history of secret societies; I have..."

"You have also seen the collection of Abraxas of the Roman prince C***, and some other closed places have been visited by you," added Désidérius in a placid tone, "I know that; it is to me that these various people had turned when they needed information, and you already found yourself my debtor ... Wait a while; I don't think I have much time left. I will give you work after my death as I have already given you during my lifetime."

And my strange companion, having relit his pipe, wished me a good night, although it was barely one o'clock in the afternoon, and disappeared into the crowd.

"What a pity," I murmured, "that such a man likes to dispose his contemporaries! In the end, I will take care of him because he must certainly have treasures in his library."

❀

Several weeks passed without seeing Désidérius again, when one morning I received a note framed in black, announcing his sudden death; there was no indication of a funeral service; only, added by hand, these simple words: Meet at the street of Champ-d'Asile at 5 am.

"So this mysterious man has connections with the F∴ M∴," I thought immediately.

At the place indicated, I found in a low room a few men, among whom I recognized Count Andréas de R., that luxurious dandy of a man who had dissipated an age-old fortune with the beautiful Stella, who has since disappeared; there was also a bearded follower of Hinduism, a bespectacled German, and one of the only representatives I have ever seen of the ancient, almost extinct race of native Chinese mountaineers, an athlete six feet high, whose penetrating eyes retained an awkward fixity.

All these people seemed to be waiting for someone; we were dressed in ceremonial clothes, which the Orientals wore with as much ease as the ex-dandy.

At the end of a moment, the door opened, giving passage to a man of high stature, whose aspect imposed attention and provoked curiosity; he seemed to me the accomplished type of Western beauty; his glance contrasted strangely with the virile aspect of all his person; one would have said the eyes of a

newborn, fresh, young, brilliant; they had this same
fixity as those of the Chinese; all the assistants greeted
him with a degree of respect, and, taking at once the
pronouncement, "We will," he said, "go at once to the
house of Désidérius, where each one will receive the
legacy indicated in the will; you know that we must go
quickly. Besides, everything must be ready."

And with these words, we left.

Half an hour later, having arrived at the home of
the deceased, the mysterious stranger opened the door
of the small property, and we found in the hallway four
enormous parcels ready to be taken away, which were
assigned to each of us.

"Here, my dear Andréas, is the whole chemical
collection of our friend: install it in our cellar; be careful
to be alone, and adjust a violet glass to your lamp
because you will find a certain number of products
that the red rays decompose; this case also contains the
books, the manuscripts, and the cryptographic keys.
Allow me to recommend patience to you.

"I have reserved for Swami the books of
physiology and psychology, where he will find the secret
shastras of Shaivism; his box also contains everything
necessary for the arrangement of an underground cell,
the gums, the varnishes, the special colors, the alluvial
earth, the black stone, and the crystal sphere.

"For you, my dear magician, here is all the
material of occult hermeneutics; the metals are
alchemically pure, the plants have been grown in
prepared soils; you will finally find the schematic rituals
of the West.

"Finally, Sir," continued the stranger, addressing me, "I have put aside for you what I thought would interest you most, that is to say, a collection of unpublished documents on the secret societies of our countries with a description of their respective teachings. A general table will give you the progress of their development; finally, if ever the desire arises in you to begin the Work a small parchment-bound notebook will show you the preparatory activities. On this note, Sir, you may, if you wish, carry away these objects and return here for the funeral ceremony."

❧

A few hours later, the six of us found ourselves taking our places in the the procession of the numerous friends of the deceased that we were leading to his final resting place. The events of that morning had plunged me into a growing surprise; all these trappings of drama could not but cast a shadow over the joy that I felt to possess at last these much-desired documents: I was boiling with impatience while waiting for the hour of solitude when I could finally see them.

That same day, after dinner, I began to unpack the box. It was hermetically filled with papers, books, and drawings; I found unknown rarities: a collection of miniatures of the time representing the Great Masters of the Temple; rolled up painted canvases, portraits of all the characters who had had a name in the history of occultism; the alchemists were there, along with the astrologers, the magicians, the Kabbalists, and the mystics. I later researched the authenticity of these paintings; experts and art critics were unanimous in their recognition. There were incunabula there, books of which collectors in the whole of Europe know only two or three copies; finally, a series of seventy-two painted pictures representing suites of geometrical figures framed in garlands of roses and of a perfect surety of execution. There were lines, circles, triangles, stars, cubes in all positions, figures of snakes as on the gnostic gems: in short, a whole obviously hermetic mess of which I understood nothing.

At this moment, I noticed that an unknown odor was floating slightly through my room; it was something like myrrh and rose oil and seemed to come from the varnish that covered the collection of seventy-two hieroglyphic paintings as well as the portraits and the book bindings; on examining this odorant varnish, I noticed that it did not flake off under the fingernail and that it seemed to be one with the substance that it protected. "It is a lost composition," I thought, "but one must find it in the books of Lemnius or Porta; we will see that later, rather in the large in-octavo of Wecker ..."

The oriental odor continued to penetrate the air gently, and I thought I felt its action on me in a very special way; it was not a numbness of the organic life, nor a disorder of physiology; my head remained free, and my pulse beat regularly; but every time I inhaled, with a puff of air, a little of this aroma, I felt in my epigastrium a sweet warmth and a kind of inner radiance, as the absorption of a generous wine could give rise to; at the same time, my muscular system was harmonized in a kind of new quietude which requires, to be understood, a few words of explanation. We have all noticed, in the course of the ordinary acts of our life, that we expend much more muscular strength than they would exactly require; we are more or less similar to the robust ploughboy who directs his plow without fatigue, but who sweats profusely when he puts his hand to the pen; in a word, we bring to each of our movements a kind of stiffness, of nervous tension, very tiring, and which disturbs the harmony of our bodily functions. This undoubtedly comes from a lack of serenity and spontaneity; civilization has dried up the free influx of nature in us; many of the most lively forms of our soul have been crumpled for centuries without number, and the atavisms of discomfort, of the restriction of all that is contrary to nature, the unnatural qualities contrary to the state of nature our cities produce upon our being, weigh as an inexorable burden on the future child who hardly ever bears our little Parisian neuroses.

This state of false tension is perceptible by the relaxation which takes place when we take the evening, or more often towards the morning, a few hours of restless sleep; the body seems to have been delivered from a constricting mold, and the millions of small cellular beings which compose it seem to enter in a repairing pause. Such are at least the impressions experienced by all those who are accustomed to observing themselves.

Now, this perfume produced on me an exactly analogous effect; all my contracted articulations seemed to relax as under the rays of a hot sun; my physical life seemed to take its amplitude again; I felt my blood beating in my veins in rhythmic waves, while an interior quivering centralized my nervous force as for some sudden and very close activity. In examining these new phenomena, my gaze wandered adventurously from my desk to my books, from the books to the lamp, and from there to the stiff whiskers of my cat, perched like a sphinx on the broad back of a cathedral; when, returning my eyes to one of these symbolic pictures, I became attached, with the same pleasure as from the contemplation of a beautiful statue, to the multicolored lines of a large star, analogous to those seen in the lodges of the Masons, bearing at their center the letter G∴, this is the sign which Faust calls the Pentagram and to which magicians attribute the most extraordinary virtues.

The one I was looking at stood out as an optical illusion against a gradient background, dark blue like the space seen by aeronauts above the region of the clouds. It was red, blue, green, yellow, and white; the unevenness of the lighting made its colors shimmer, and it literally charmed me as any object enchants the dreams of the user of hashish. Around my pentagram flamed, on the dark blue background, the letters of a circular inscription written in an unknown language; it was neither Sanskrit, Hebrew, Arabic, nor Tibetan, nor any of the Hindu dialects; I did not remember having seen similar ones in the *Steganography* nor in the *Polygraphy* of that son of Trittenheim called, inappropriately, Trithemius, who is said to have belonged to the most mysterious societies of his time. Perhaps it was one of the secret idioms of India: the Parvi or the Senzar; no doubt the manuscripts would give me the key, and I was already beginning to apply mentally to this sentence the first rules of cryptography when an interior tremor resounded in me, I felt my life, condensed into a globe; I was in deep darkness, I heard two or three chords of an admirable harmony; a luminous point opened in front of me like an iridescent diaphragm and I found myself in violet light, on the slabs of a low room where heavy and bitter fumes were floating.

I did not have the idea to inquire about the modus operandi by which I was brought to this unexpected scene; the spectacle that I contemplated interested me powerfully and centralized all the forces of my being.

I was not alone: I counted three men dressed in black robes and five women in pale green tunics. At the back of the room, I discerned a sort of low pyramid formed of seven steps; two meters above it there shone, with a motionless brightness, a small violet light; each man was between two women, and the eight characters were arranged on a triangle whose point was the small pyramid; the men rested each of their arms on the shoulders of their companions; they had in front of them tripods with burning berries and white resins; behind us, on the ground, one had laid out an uninterrupted line of pine cones.

I tried to distinguish the faces of my chance companions; they were of all ages, but a certain uniformity of type bound them together. The men were thin, tall, and of sorrowful aspect; there were three

women of extraordinary beauty; brunette, pale, the
figure frozen, the eyes closed; they raised, in a statuary
immobility, faces of suffering and despondency. What
unspeakable pains did they have to bear? From the
weight of what sins did they not seem to falter? In the
two older ones, life no longer seemed to be in their
bodies but took refuge entirely in their faces; in the folds
of the pale mouths was resignation; on the unwrinkled
foreheads, the single light of an unshakeable firmness;
in the eyes, the splendor of secret sacrifice; and I was
sinking into a somewhat fearful astonishment, when
suddenly – for I had retained what moderns call full
consciousness in the waking state – the three men
began to utter rhythmic phrases. Ah, what a mystery
their voices were!

They spoke in unison, in a sonorous, dull, lulling
language; listening to them, I imagined a bronze
forged by the Kobolds, with the cries, pains, and
sighs of men; a hard and burning metal, fluid and
vibrating, which would sound the knells of low agony,
the hiccups of a tortured heart, the slow anguish, the
fears without reason, like a gong where would pass the
complaint of the winter wind, the howls of the sea,
or the awful silence of the haunted moors. Ah, here
is the cry of a victim of the Inquisition; here is the
moan of a deceived heart; here is the complaint of a
tortured man from the East; here is the horror of a soul
beset by demons! And each word rebounded on my
being, tearing me, consulting me, making me cry for
mercy towards the immobile and frozen enchanters.
Instead of the respite I had hoped for, the voices of

the five women served to heighten my distress. They sang at intervals, giving color and livid flashes to the monotonous and vertiginous engraving produced by the men. The music was also foreign and indefinable; it obsessed me, and, implacable in its complaint, it got the better of the attitude of distrust that I had taken from the beginning of this singular dream. I dropped my prejudice, and at once, the mysterious symbols entered my soul and stripped themselves there, but with what lively energy, with what cruel vehemence, with what heartbreaking sharpness! Having reached the gates of the grave, I still do not think without shuddering of this night of my mature age. The song of these women stood in the high notes of supplication and penitence; then the dark space before my eyes lit up with a sparkle of stars, or a purple flash of lightning crossed corners of shadow; it was then a distraught soul, wracked in its entrails, the inexpressible despair of an eternal farewell to loved ones, and the flame of the incense-burners became alive; it rose up straight like the humble and pure repentance of the sinner or it twisted like the pain of a being tormented by demons. Ah! The awful pictures of burning brimstone and pitch, described by the monotonous murmur of the priests, illuminated by the reddened irons, the streams of molten lead, the wicked gems of the painful voices; the sensation of foul and viscous contacts where all the lustful leprosy of mankind sticks, the spectral faces of cynicism and vice appeared on the black velvet of the suffocating air; all the horror of the monastic nightmares was certainly there, overwhelmed me to the point of nausea and made me cry out for mercy, was going to beat me to the impassive actors, when a silence fell that was more frightening in its nakedness than the inexpressible ugliness of these ghosts; the flames of the incense-burners flattened towards the interior of the triangle, and, with the dazzling light that the small violet lamp threw before going out, I saw at my feet the body of Désidérius; I did not have any more the strength to resist, when the assistants threw themselves down, dragging me with them, face down, my almost-held breath caressing the face of the dead man; a sensation of extraordinary fluid crossed my spine, horror entered my being, my teeth clashed convulsively, an electric crackling was heard at the same time in the four corners of the room. I saw blood gushing from the mouth of the corpse, and I lost consciousness. I mean that the whole scene disappeared from before my eyes as my room had done.

It seemed to me that I had lost my body, or rather each of my faculties had received an autonomous life, and each of my emotions, each of my desires flew away from me like an angel of jubilation; I swam at the bottom of a sea of sweetness and rest, with the intuition of a resplendent sun, on the road on which all my aspirations preceded me by opening the way. The mysterious operators of the nocturnal room surrounded me, transfigured and delighted, and we followed in silent joy, the soul of Désidérius clothed with science and will, going to collect in the light of glory the price of its works.

It seemed to me to guess the enigma of the

Universe; with a vertiginous speed, I saw the sights of my life again; I penetrated the sense of them, and I conceived the perpetual and vivifying action of God in nature; the men with whom I spoke formerly – as everything was far away – appeared to me like animated bowls, revelators of a divine will; they were myself and, in each one of them, one of the faculties of my soul recognized itself with admiration.

Suddenly, a dazzling flash of lightning: I am blinded; I pass again in a fulguration in the darkened room; it is my study with its lamp which burns; the small clock does not work anymore: the cat is in catalepsy; the same subtle odor floats in the air, and I literally die of hunger and fatigue. I try to get up from the couch where this strange dream surprised me, my hands beat the air to help the impotent effort of my legs, and their feverish gesture brings back the small black notebook, which the stranger had recommended I read. On the first page, a beautiful calligrapher's handwriting traced a title: Letters of Théophane (Θεοφάνη) to Stella.

Théophane! The one who sees God! I will not recount all the reflections I made the following day; they led me into complex adventures which had a considerable influence on the rest of my life; as I estimate nothing better in the world than the charm of an active and eventful life, I believe I am doing the public a service (or rather that small part of the public which knows how to remove the kernel from its bitter envelope) by giving it knowledge of these letters. Let the readers use each one for the best, and I think that they will draw some profit from their study.

ℒETTER I

ANDRÉAS TO STELLA

You have always shown yourself, my dear Stella, as a sure soul unafraid of the blows of Destiny; this is why you will be the first to know the one that I have just received from this master of the world. I am broke; metals, which had hitherto had some sympathy for my hands, have suddenly changed their taste and left me in almost complete destitution. You know me well enough to know that I will not seek the compassion of my friends or, rather, of my comrades at feasts. It is without any regret that I leave them; we have too often noticed together their small-mindedness and pettiness in not wishing greater decoration to our pride.

What I miss is the beautiful architecture, the pure forms of marble, the tasteful paintings that will have to be abandoned to the hazards of fortune; they are the supple hangings, the silverware, the delicate crystal, the heroic armor that call the chances of an adventurous destiny among rich and barbarous foreigners; all these magnificent forms, I loved them as images of my mind, as foils of your beauty, my dear Stella; like elixirs of eternal youth for the sensitivity of my taste and for the delicate emotions of our brains. But everything passes here below, and if, in the flower of my age, Destiny threw me among the poor wretches and the vanquished, I who nevertheless never fought, it is apparently for some secret and childish reason, like all those who behave as men. Perhaps I am going to pass through this terrible crucible of misery and hunger to come out of it weakened to the point of cowardice, drunk with solitary pride, or transformed to the point of genius? Don't these predictions amuse you? I see your beautiful smile and all the harmony in your body. I must also say goodbye to this masterpiece. Couldn't I greet it one last night, Stella, before sinking into the cold darkness into which fate has thrown me?

ℒETTER II

ANDRÉAS TO STELLA

I have been touched, my dearest friend, and perhaps for the first time since my young years when the breath of the twilight wind filled me with a secret terror. Your letter made me feel love, that butterfly after which the extravagant Andréas ran in vain and which the miserable and fallen Andréas found. I thought I owed your affection only to a bit of science borrowed from the erotic books of a certain Nguyen pagoda, and here the unreal flame of another love gleams in your heart. How beautiful you must have been when you wrote this letter that I want to keep as the only relic I have left of you and of our beautiful years! No, I don't want to do what you say, and even though we should have covered with a mantle of correctness what of your offer would have been shocking to the common man, I won't accept it. You know that I have always been a bit of a poet, that is to say, a bit of a madman; why should I shrink from my destiny? Why should I fear it? If pride was, during my days of happiness, the elixir which made my joys more subtle and higher, it would be, in my distress, the stick which would remove the stone from my foot and the aggressor from my road. Also, I do not fear anything, dear Stella. And in everything, do not see in my refusal the retreat of a wounded vanity: we are both, I think, of a higher and simpler breed, which only wants to know divine feelings. Stay in your splendor; continue to shine on the dazzled crowd with some reflections of your Beauty. For me, I take your image, the splendid memory of your body, the perpetual vision of your attitudes of voluptuousness, the savor of your flesh. Do you believe that this treasure of life is not worth the cold copies of Art?

But, after all, I begin to think that all things are true; the artists in love with the artificial and the monstrous undoubtedly borrow their conceptions from some internal reality, as the lovers of life are inspired by the spectacles of the external nature; but who will say where the external begins, where the internal ends? What dreams have we not lived in our nights of voluptuousness? Where were we? What were we exactly?

As you felt the fine fabric of your nerves stretching in the room, as your hallucinating eyes lost, in a light vapor which seemed to come out of it, the contours of your body, so your mind opened to ideas foreign to the meditations of women; in prey to the intoxication of Eros, you felt yourself becoming such an object which, during the day, had stopped your glance; you suffered the pains of the rose that your fine fingers pick in the morning, you sang with the young birds of your aviary, happy to find their mistress; and, imitating the motionless meditation of our cats with large eyes, you felt the hidden forces of the Universe descending in your bosom or you discovered, in the shadowy corners of the room, the dancing silhouette of a familiar spirit.

Dear Stella, these ghosts [apparitions] were real because you saw them; was it the heavy perfumes of India that gave them a body? Or did the rhythmic themes of the dances I taught you develop unknown forces in the air, as is the will of our modern scholars, as superstitious Orientals believe? Perhaps the complicated rites that the priests of the pagodas teach for love are really effective in exalting the lovers into unutterable ecstasies? Isn't everything plausible? And why, when you say, "No, it is not"? To deprive oneself of pleasure or an idea, perhaps?

Well, then, my friend, I will go to the party you are going to give me. We will tell our comrades, our parasites, that I am going on a very long journey for an indefinite time, and I will take a memory of you in my miserable solitude, a memory of splendor and beauty.

Your love is worth sharing my plans with you, as your discretion is that of a man, and I beg you to keep absolutely silent about this and about the news you may receive from me afterward. From my travels in the East, I have brought back the knowledge of someone on whom I count from now on; of my relations with this man, I will tell you nothing because these secrets do not belong to me. I have always followed with interest the life of stones, and you have often heard me suppose that gems, pearls, and the most obscure minerals are unknown beings who are born, live, love, and die. I will, since I have nothing else to do, continue the study which has always fascinated me; perhaps you will see me again, an old shaggy alchemist, surrounded by retorts, but more surely, you will see me the day after tomorrow to admire you one last time. You will also see that evening the friend whom I have just talked to you about and whom we will call Théophane if you wish; he will be a sober and noisy guest.

See you soon, dear Stella, the most precious of my works of art, the rarest of my old treasures.

ℒETTER III

ANDRÉAS TO STELLA

Alas, dear Stella, I could not help feeling sad for the last eight days, thinking that I had lost you; how delicious our last night was, how the pain of an imminent separation sharpened all our voluptuousness! We carried each other to the gates of death, and together we suffered the terrible and delicious shiver of Azrael's presence. But I am wrong to remember these adorable moments; it is eight long days and eight longer nights that I have been fighting against their dreadful memory. For you, at least, the favorable sky will give you commemorations of our fervor, full of charms, while your unfortunate lover, doomed to solitude, will only have to console himself with the spectacle of the marriage of liquid metals in the crucibles of his laboratory. But my melancholy makes me forget all propriety, and I neglect to inform you about the subjects that interest you. I suspected that the appearance of my friend would not leave you indifferent, and not to hide anything from you, I counted on him to distract you from your pain.

Since you are so charmingly insistent, I will tell you the details of my first meeting with Théophane; I am also very happy to be able to prolong my conversation with you; you know how weak we are when it comes to carrying out the rules we have set for ourselves. I have already told you that about ten years ago, I was walking on the northern slopes of the mountains which separate the two empires of China and Siam. This region, still unknown, had tempted me because of the legends which ran about it; endless forests, splendid landscapes, impetuous rivers, exuberant flora and fauna, the tiger to hunt: so many motives which consolidated me in my resolution.

I was then in Rangoon, where I was resting from my peregrinations in India, preparing my next trip in a sweet idleness. I must confess to an act of skepticism from which the religiosity of the West, so lukewarm though it is, always deviates a little. I had noticed the extreme courtesy of the Eastern peoples towards Europeans and their haughtiness toward their inferiors; on the other hand, their insouciance of death and danger indicated to me that this politeness was all superficial and dictated by other feelings than fear; I believed that it came from their pride and from the conscience of their superiority over us. But where does this superiority lie? I could not find out. I then made a very simple decision: I was in the middle of a Buddhist population, and I resolved to become a Buddhist. I already spoke the language of the country; in addition, I learned Pali, to read in the ancient manuscripts the words of the Sublime; I made myself accustomed to walk barefoot and to contain my attitude and my gaze; I made, one beautiful day after having sent back all my paraphernalia of an explorer, profession between the hands of a dozen priests. I quickly became accustomed to the simple life of the religious beggar; with the resulting impossibility of following all the prejudices which regulate the clothing, the food, and the life of the European in these regions, I felt myself becoming young again; the physical well being, the freedom of my senses, the vivacity of my intelligence, all grew in notable portions. I was resolved to give religious studies only the strict time necessary to preserve my disguise; I realized after a week that I had undertaken very complicated work. Credulous like all travelers, I believed that the Siamese monks were indolent, lazy, and unoccupied; don't all Orientalists represent them as knowing only the few prayer formulas required by their functions? I was quickly disabused of this notion. Each novice is attached to the service of a Prefect for at least a year. The one to whom I was assigned was a man of about forty years of age, sympathetic and of the calm exterior like all his brothers. He was one of the few blessed minds to whom a smile was habitual, as usually these monks had an absorbed and somber expression. He spoke to me in the tone of the clergymen of our countries, an amusing resemblance; add to that a rather strong build and heady expressiveness: you will then have, my dear friend, a sketch of the one whom I called my Lord and for whom I washed his feet several times a day. Everything went well for the first week; I got up before the sun to do my ablutions and to walk in the courtyard of the monastery; I never found again the impression of lightness and peace that the whole surrounding forest gave off; the rest of the day was spent under this penetrating charm and the evening reading still found me in a restful quietude. In spite of that, I did not lose sight of my travel plans; all I needed for their execution was the delivery of a mission to the northeast and a defensive weapon of some sort. The first point was to be naturally presented; it was the time when France was beginning to conquer Tonkin; and, something unknown to our diplomats, these hostilities had stirred up the whole northern border of Indo-China; as for the reasons for these extraordinary worries among these peoples so different in race, language, and religion, I have never been able to know them.

Still, our Siamese Buddhists were in constant correspondence with monasteries lost north of the mountain. There were constructions to be built there, active works, to which I was recognized as being very willing, more especially as the religious state prescribed an exemplary wisdom of which I would never have been capable without the close monitoring of my brothers and without great muscular fatigue. When I left, my preceptor addressed a little speech to me in which he expressed in veiled terms, with wishes and advice, that he was not very sure of the perfect sincerity of my Buddhist convictions; and, as astonished by his penetration, I protested of my fervor: "That's good, my son," he said, smiling and with lowered eyes, "but why do you seek poison?"

I was stunned, for he was right; I was really trying to make a blowpipe in secret for my tiger hunts and to kill a variety of vipers whose venom is lightning; I had not breathed a word to anyone of my project; in an instant, all manner of hypotheses presented themselves to my mind; I thought he had spied on me. I denied it with all possible composure; he listened to me in silence and answered, "My son, lying is suicide; but you still have to live in the world before you see the light; go to the mountain since your destiny calls you there; you will learn there how he who has freed himself from the twelve chains penetrates the thoughts of others."

I will spare you the account of my journey; all travelers' accounts are similar, and you know for yourself the beauties of the oriental flora; but you do not know the scourges of these walks: mosquitoes and poisonous beasts. By a singular chance, in two months of walking, through all kinds of countries, forests, jungles, clearings, scrub, rocks, and swamps, not one of us was bitten by a snake or stung by a fly.

I will pass over the details of our arrival and the construction of the Vihara; I was beginning to find the time long, and I was combining my travel plans, the best of which was very impractical; we were on the eastern slope of Indo-China; therefore, by following any one of the many streams that watered the mountain, I would certainly arrive in the middle of Annam in a few weeks. We lived on a grassy plateau completely surrounded by a forest of multiplying trees; the air was dry, aromatic, and charged with electricity; also, according to the Scriptures, our superior had ordered us to make a strict retreat, and, as the only one in the community, I was allowed to go out to harvest the fruits necessary for the sustenance of all. I was entirely taken by the magic of the site and by the certain charm that comes from a community of wills united toward the same ideal.

One day in the forest, jumping over a wormy trunk, the noise I made awakened one of those little flat-headed vipers I was looking for; it reared up faster than lightning; my gaze met its round, staring eyes, and it slithered away at full speed. Instantly, the hunter resurrected in me; I rushed after it, jumping to my feet; I crushed its head with my heels. I immediately collected the venom from its reservoirs and, having cleaned a hollow stone; I deposited it there; then I returned to the monastery, determined to leave that very evening.

Happily, I was able to carry out my plan, and as soon as the moon was visible through the broad leaves of the fig trees, I set out, dressed in the yellow robe under which I hid my blowpipe and arrows, carrying the alms-box and armed with great confidence in my star. The enterprise was reckless; on the part of those whom I was leaving, I had nothing to fear, but I was going to expose myself to every danger in a country infested with ferocious beasts. The rapid slopes which descend from the mountains are indeed an inextricable thicket of high grass, thorny bushes, and rocks, where tigers lie in great numbers. I began to hear them from the fifth night of walking, and, to get some sleep, I had to climb a large tree every time the sun set, relying on my good fortune to avoid either the encounter of a scorpion in the hollow of the wood or the risk of being discovered on a large branch by one of these terrible man-eaters.

Towards the middle of the sixth day, I discovered from the top of a rock a thin stream of water flowing in the low meadow; I ran to it with joy because I had not drunk since my departure, and my thirst quenched; I followed it, persuaded that it would lead me somewhere towards the East; I also used the landmarks, and in the night the stars, the positions of which I had asked the Buddhists. My stream increased little by little; one fine day, I saw it form a small waterfall; its course became faster; I wanted to make use of it; I built myself a kind of narrow raft with vines and leaves, which I replaced every day. I broke a young tree of two to three meters which served me as rudder and oar, and I embarked carelessly on rough and rather fast water.

One of the following days, I saw a tall man driving an ox; I could not stop because of the violence of the current. A few hours later, an unknown noise made me prick up my ears, and it resembled rather that of the sea on the breakers; very distant at first, it increased abruptly at a bend of the river; my heart tightened; I had recognized a rapid; too inexperienced to have confidence in the handling of my sculling, I thought myself lost, provided the waterfall was high. Nothing to do: the two banks were suddenly encased in walls of granite; the noise became deafening, and I went much faster than a galloping horse. I saw a bar of foam forming in front of the rocks at the water level; I closed my eyes and clung to my raft. The sensation of a fall, a bruise, a plunge; I find myself at the bottom of calmer water, I go back up with a desperate kick of the heel, and I arrive exhausted on a spit of sand, where I lose consciousness.

I was brought back to consciousness by a sharp

pain that tore my back; I felt a huge weight suffocating me, a stinking breath suffocated me; I guessed with terror, because I had fallen face down, that a tiger was on me; it did not hurry. I felt his rough tongue licking the blood that flowed from my arm; I saw, with the lightning speed of agony, an arrow coming out of my clothing, the tiger stung and killing me in its spasm of death. I wanted to take the chance: slowly, with my crimson skin, I folded my arm, seized an arrow and took it out, and was preparing to turn sideways to see my enemy, whose flank must have been within my reach, when he gave a frightful roar and crouched over my body, sinking his claws into my flesh. I thought I would die of pain; in a convulsion I turned my head violently and saw a tall man coming slowly out of the wood and approaching the shore, his arms glued to his body and his gaze riveted on the tiger; I was dying of suffocation, pain, weakness, and anger; I had this arm which held the arrow crushed by a paw of the animal, I felt its claws piercing and releasing my living flesh; after a few seconds, a great lassitude invaded me, I forgot the suffering, I looked at my situation as a spectator. I saw the man approaching slowly; he had an admirable musculature, and he seemed to me gigantic; I savored all his physical perfection with complete serenity; "How is it," I said to myself, "that he wears his beard? He is not from this country." I wanted to see his face better, but my exhaustion made me see before his eyes a purple cloud, through which passed the fire of his clear eyes. The tiger continued to growl deafeningly, and I could hear its powerful tail beating the earth with the sound of a flail on the hard ground. The man was a few steps away from us; I felt the tiger's claws go deeper; he was about to jump, but a shiver ran down its skin; it gave a high-pitched mewl; the man was there and put one hand over its eyes and the other over its muzzle; The animal's legs trembled, the terrible muscles relaxed, the claws left the red sheaths they had dug into my flesh, the terrible weight that had been suffocating me was lifted from my chest, the ferocious beast crawled away at the feet of my savior, its head flattened, its ears lowered like a dog under the threat of the whip; I saw it disappear little by little into the deep thickets.

The man took me in his arms, washed me in the river, and applied to my wounds the leaves of a small plant, binding them with green and flexible vines. — You have guessed that this tamer was Théophane; the rest of our story is not interesting; let me hope now that the unknown will not disturb your sleep, which I hope will be deep and lulled with beautiful dreams.

Write to me, dear Stella; I love you more and more every day.

𝒬ETTER IV

ANDRÉAS TO STELLA

I sensed that my curious friend would be interested in the silent guest of her last party; I can't remember without smiling the arrival of Théophane in the elegant crowd that crowded into your palace. Brown beauties and blond beauties, dandies in the style of Lord Byron style, young gods in tail coats, great ruined lords, they all felt the presence of an Unknown; the smiles were frozen, the paradoxes expired, and the voluptuous desires died for a second, while the great height of Théophane bowed to whisper in your ear words that must have moved you. And for a good moment, the whole swarm of your laughing guests contemplated in silence the face, the body, the attitude, and the manners of the new arrival; then they communicated to each other in whispers the results of their examination. "He looks like an athlete," said the first. "He looks like," said the other, who prides herself on erudition, "the Assyrian bas-relief in the Louvre Museum, where we see a man holding a lion under his arm." "He is an old man," exclaimed the third. "He has the Evil Eye," shivered an Italian. "He touched me in passing," confessed a blushing blonde, while my dear Stella regained, as if by virtue of a powerful potion, more splendor, radiance, and charm than she had ever possessed.

You want to see Théophane again, my poor friend, and you think you are only giving in to the childish curiosity that one has for a strange gypsy woman; astrology and palmistry are very beautiful sciences, certainly, and he is, it seems, a great expert in them; but beware! If you knew to what pains you run, to what sorrows you run, to what hardships you devote yourself, to what humiliations you subscribe, the obscure desire which rises in you, the pale gleam of your secret intuition would flee, frightened by the boldness of their project. Ah! Why don't you stay in the brilliant sphere where Fate has placed you; reckless seeker, how will you be able to live in solitude and in pain? For you will love him, this man of whom you are curious; you will be initiated into the secrets of the heart; and you will buy these secrets with all your beauty, with your blood, with your very life. Poor Stella! You will, while reading my words, believe me jealous; it is not your body that he will take, he will invent for you neither new caresses, nor words of a superhuman tenderness; woe to you if he doesn't love you, but even more woe if he does; his love is a devouring fire; you will suffer by him all the agonies; it is, at least as they say down there in the secret crypts, the only way open to a woman to arrive at the Way.

Dear Stella, over whom I will weep, you will see Théophane and he will undoubtedly speak to you. Farewell, this time, for a long time.

ꝒETTER V

THÉOPHANE TO STELLA

Y ou came running, Stella, where you thought
I was, and behind the heavy door, alone, the
voice of a rabid dog answered you. See how
external things are the exact symbol of internal things.
Are you not today, in the midst of your luxury, your
parties and your courtiers, like a poor abandoned
creature, who anxiously seeks his master, who thinks
he is always recognizing him and who falls back from
disillusionment to secret despair, losing little by little
even the courage to rise again, while the echoes of
your pain are the only answers you receive from all this
vast universe which seems to have never known you.

Don't believe it, however; on the contrary,
a multitude without number of attentive and
sympathetic eyes look at your misery and sympathize
with it. The external world, which is all you have
glimpsed until now, with its highest forms and most
splendid magnificences, is only a pale reflection, only
a coarse and corrupted envelope of other purer and
more beautiful worlds; these unknown spheres are
populated by prestigious beings who, like the daughters
of Jerusalem the Holy, are the pitying spectators of
your errors, of your struggle in the darkness, and of
your sufferings. Ah! If your body is beautiful, your soul
is also, but only by the attraction of its tears; you were

nothing until this day, but an instrument of lust, that a pretext of covetousness and greed; however, this vile matter hides the germ of the diamond which you will become perhaps one day.

This secret darkness where you wander, it is not only outside of you, it is also within you; it oppresses you, tortures you, overwhelms you mysteriously; kisses have no more flavor, fingers get tired of the caress of fabrics and eyes of the wonders of art; within you kneels, laments, and sobs a veiled weeper suffocated by tears. Look at this weeping woman, listen to her lament, Stella; it is the form that has taken, for you, the one who stands at the center of the world like the pole of a tent, the formidable Architect who sculpts stones with lightning; the one who takes matter in the hollow of his hand, who crushes it there and who makes long bloody spurts of it spout out from between his pitiless fingers. He is motionless while the spheres revolve around him; he is mute, but his eyes distribute lightning to the four corners of the world; he is invisible, but the palaces he builds are splendid outside and dark inside.

Don't hate this worker, Stella, bless his hand and wish to feel again and again the tearing of his nails.

ℒETTER VI

THÉOPHANE TO STELLA

Do not look for consolation outside; the visible realities exist but are not. You think to find the cure for your malady and forget your anguish in the practice of luxuriousness and voluptuousness; you feel, however, well in yourself, that you emptied the delicious liquor and that at the bottom of the cup the bitter dregs remains for you only to drink. Listen to the little voice that whispers imperceptibly in your heart. Do not show yourself, hide yourself; do not rise, lower yourself; do not look for the sun, but for the night; for you are hidden, and the icy fire of the night star is the only elixir that can give you a new life.

Go within yourself and see the marvelous chain of events of your existence, the invisible wisdom of their succession. What is today your self has gone through the immense cycle of innumerable existences; it has been the latent fire that hides in the silent pebble; then the molecule of earth from which a modest grass has drawn some of its sap; a precious jewel, it has shone for weeks of centuries on the chests of ancient dancers or on the foreheads of majestic hierophants. But the wrath of the cosmic powers unleashed on the universe where it lived cataclysms of water and fire; precipitated again into the confused ocean of primitive germs, it emerged elevated by a kingdom in the physical hierarchy. This atom of vital fire has taken on the various forms of roots, herbs, flowers, and fruits; it has been an obscure worker buried in the bosom of the earth, a shining cell of petals, a grain of perfumed pollen, a centenarian and venerable tree, millions of times it has seen the sun being born and dying at the opposite points of the horizon; for countless ages it has received the lessons of the fairies, dryads, and fauns. Here it is plunged back into the great vegetable sea, from where the new breath of the spirit makes it re-emerge as a spontaneous creature, free in its movements, to whom the deep mass of the waters, the surface of the green earth and the azure space of the air were successively allotted. Your body, Stella, is a summary of the whole creation; motionless, it is an elegant palm tree; your walk has borrowed, from the sacred snakes which stood near the perfume burners, the perfidy of their undulations; your hair is the silky and warm down of some swan of Australia; your lips are a red corolla wet with dew; your nails are corals polished by the ceaseless caress of the great Thalassa; your eyes are gems refined in the subterranean crucibles of the gnomes; your voice is the morning hymn of the birds; in the depths of your heart, finally, is lurking some voluptuous and cruel panther altered by lust and blood.

Such is the inferior Stella, such is the unconscious form which, until now, dispensed on the crowd the seeds of crimes and perversities. This little will-o'-the-wisp, drunk with its freedom and false light, has populated its sphere with extravagance and revolt; it did not feel the hand of the great Harmony, measuring its deviations, and dispensing, according to the norm, the proportions of its activities; thus a living fire attached itself to your bosom, consuming unceasingly the vile matters of your being, and bringing you down little by little from the joyous realm to the realm of sorrow.

Thus, this world, which your multiple beauties subjugated, shook little by little the flexible chains that your seductions had forged to it. The lower your imperious charm made your fathers prostrate themselves at your feet, the more consumingly burns in their heart the unconscious hatred that they nourish against you. The star that has shone sees its body reduced to ashes when the Being of Beings withdraws His breath from it.

When the Eternal One threw into the womb of the celestial Mother the little germ which is you and which has been, since the beginning of the ages, the ever-young witness of its own transformations, He gave it, out of the vast Universe, a little world to govern. This world is your name, dear ignorant sister, which was given to you in the beginning, which has protected you in all your falls, and which will be your garment of glory in your future exaltation. This little cosmos in which you are queen, you were given the mission to guard it, to cultivate it and to watch over its productions. These were your mystical sons, on whom a mother's tender solicitude should have been bent, and from whom the seductions of the ancient serpent made you turn your eyes away.

ꟐETTER VII

ANDRÉAS TO STELLA

Let me, Stella, rock the little perpetual pain that nestles in your soul, let me tell you fairy tales. Don't be surprised that I know, without having seen you, the state you are in. Didn't I tell you, some time ago, that I was beginning to love you? And if you remember that, in the past, the delicious weariness of our caresses loosened, in our home, the heavy chains of physical matter, you will understand how, if my heart dashes towards yours, it feels, as if it were yours, the palpitations of life and the roughness of the rock by means of which you ascend the sides of the mysterious mountain.

Once upon a time, there was a poor shepherd who seemed an innocent; he looked after the sheep of the inhabitants of a small village lost in the depths of the Black Forest, much deeper and much more deserted at that time than now. This little shepherd, whose name was Hans, did not know his parents; he had arrived, as a child, in this village, whose inhabitants, simple and good, had taken him in; but as soon as he was old enough to know his way along the barely-marked paths that crossed the immense forest, he was employed to lead to the pastures of the mountains the small flock that constituted the main fortune of these poor people. Hans had a strange life; he was seen very little: barely in the morning at the time he crossed the road blowing his horn, and in the evening putting his cattle back in their stables; he spoke little, with an absent air, and at night, instead of sleeping in the good fresh straw of the barns or under the warm breath of the cattle in the winter, he wandered in the forest, with his face stretched out towards the moon and the stars, and the good people believed him to be a bit of a wizard.

He had been seen, in the midst of the high forests, listening to hidden voices, smiling at invisible spectacles; the Forest seemed to give him lessons; he knew the weather by inspecting the gaps of blue sky seen through the foliage; he learned little-by-little which herbs made bruises disappear, dried wounds, or healed cattle; the crow and the owl even spoke to him, and when Death visited this lost hamlet, he knew in advance on which hut it would stop. Thus Hans grew up happily, in the fragrant breaths of the forest; the flowers of summer, the fruits and the golden horizons of autumn, the carpet of the winter snows followed one another many times without him knowing any other feelings than admiration and peace.

He had only friends among the trees and grasses because he had never harmed any of them; before picking a fruit, pulling out a root, cutting a stem, he had always asked permission from the person concerned concerned, and when he was looking for good juicy leaves to dress a wound, he never stripped the little shrub of its own authority. He would go through the forest, asking loudly, "Where are the St. John's wort?" or this and that plant, and he would add, "Who is the one who will give me a few leaves to heal old Gretel, or to stop the blood from a cut that Fritz the carpenter has made?" Then a little shrub would answer, "That's me, take what you need from my leaves, but don't hurt me too much." So as not to hurt friends, little Hans would wait until they were asleep under the moon; and when all the children of the forest were dozing peacefully, he would take his leaves from the one who had offered them to him, very gently, making as few tears as possible and carefully closing the green scar. So everyone loved him and was happy to give him what he asked for.

At least Hans claimed that it was so; and the people of the village listened to him with astonishment because they had never heard the voice of a shrub; when they told him such things, the little shepherd was indeed a little astonished, but as he was a simple child and full of respect for old men and old women, he took no glory from his forest relationships and did not seek the cause. Every day, however, he learned something wonderful from his friends the trees, and he told it to his friends the men, thinking it would be useful to them, as he described to the trees the ways of the peasants; but the trees alone listened seriously to him and profited by the lessons of their friend, because they were humble and knew that man is far superior to them; but the peasants said of Hans, "He is a simple man, nixies cloud his mind," and they forgot his warnings and many times paid dearly for their indisposition. For trees sense many things that men, even rustic people, do not sense: they know what the weather will be like, not only many days but also many moons in advance; the giants of the forest even predict these things for future years; they also know the mysterious presences that fill the traveler with dread under the canopies of dark greenery; those of them who live on the edges of the round glades where the fairies come to dance on the sixth, thirteenth, twentieth, and twenty-seventh days of the moon are the most knowledgeable; If men knew how to listen to them and asked them, they would put them in touch with the geniuses of the meadows, the streams, the waterfalls, the rocks, the ravines, and the mountains; then one would learn the places where the gnomes work the useful grounds, the invaluable ores, where the undines dispense to the springs a medicinal virtue, where the flowers are balsamic; one would know that such a centenarian was blessed by the austerities of a hermit, that such other is haunted by the memory of a crime or the torments of a suicide, and many other things still.

But, like the civilized and learned people, the good farmers among whom Hans lived paid no attention to his stories, and even laughed at them among themselves. The white frost or hail always came when the little shepherd said it would, but these lessons did not benefit them, because it was a kind of little vagrant who fell from who-knows-where who gave them.

Now, one fine afternoon, Hans, walking through an undergrowth covered with creeping ivy, saw its leaves not standing perpendicular to the sun's rays, as they should have been, but presenting themselves to them by the edge, and he knew at once that he had been drawn to that corner because something important was about to befall him; the ivy, which sees the bad humors of animal bodies, did not want to obey the Law that day, and Hans felt cold at heart. When his flock returned, he ran under the moonlight to the great oak Arra'ch, the Master of the Forest, but it was a night of Council, and Arra'ch had gone at the head of the tree spirits to take orders and receive news from the mouth of the old bear, through whom many of the Genii of that ancient land spoke. So it was only towards morning that Hans heard in his dream the voice of Arra'ch: "You will suffer," he said to him, "and whatever you do you will grow; you will be forced to choose between two roads: to taste, of two fruits the one, and to throw away the other; but you must choose by yourself; I can do nothing for you, because you are a man; your Spirit is higher than mine, and if one chooses wisely, he will one day become the master of this forest, my master, the master of the old bear and the master of the gnomes who work in the rocks to the north. But as you have been good to us, we will be with you, and I pledge, in the name of the whole Forest, to help you if you do not forget us." And Hans heard the immense murmur of the great trees, the shrubs, the grasses that swore with their master Arra'ch loyalty to Hans, if Hans did not forget them.

It must be said that the little shepherd had become a handsome blond teenager; straight and vigorous like a young shoot, and whose good looks did not go unnoticed by the girls of the hamlet. But he had never noticed their blushing smiles; they were for him only comrades, less agile and less bold than the boys. Now, a few days after he had seen the leaves of the sylvan ivy rise up before him, there arrived in the village an unknown brunette girl, with large, still eyes, broad hips and long hair. Hans, at the sight of her, felt something tremble in his chest, and his nostrils, accustomed to the fresh and pure odors of the herbs and the white ladies, experienced the dizziness of the scents of the flesh. In his trouble he went to his usual advisers; but the Forest was silent to him that night, and the master Arra'ch said to him, "It is just now that you must choose."

The dark-haired girl spoke to him, since he did not dare to do so; she came from a neighboring region where there was no forest, where men lived together in great numbers, living not in huts but in stone structures; they had complicated customs and many clothes; many objects were necessary to them to eat, to sleep, to look after their body, and the stranger was astonished not to find similar ones in the hamlet; Hans told her of his life, his friends, his masters, the trees, his guides, the fairies, their speeches and their predictions; he wanted his new friend to speak to them, but she did not hear their voice, nor would she have understood their voice, for her spirit came from another realm. Then she mocked Hans, and Hans suffered from her sarcasm, though he breathed with delight the breath of the brown hair girl and the oppressive perfume of her body; she wanted to take him to live among these men whom she said were learned, powerful, and rich;

but Hans did not know what wealth was; he had an idea of what a learned man is. He wanted to learn secret, distant and obscure things, and among them the enigma that he felt was hidden in the beauty of his friend; but he did not dare to leave his Forest; he felt that he would lose many things there. He did not believe either that he could live without the caress of the dark eyes, without the delicious and somewhat disturbing smell, without the sight of the beautiful body of the Unknown. So he was worried until one day, suddenly, putting his hand in the temptress' hand, he left for the unknown city, to know wealth and learn science.

He wanted to learn the secret held by the red lips of his friend; but she rejected him, saying, "Come back when you have gold and you will discover the mystery of my beauty." When he had gold, he knew this mystery, he used it up and got tired of it; he also knew it in many other women and got tired of it. He then sought out the mysteries of science. He learned many forgotten things, the languages of vanished peoples, the dreams of the ancient sages; but the word of the mystery of science he could not pronounce; one day he thought he would never be able to discover it, and then he realized that he had become old, that his hands were trembling, that his hair had turned white. So he returned to his old forest, and in the hamlet where he had spent his childhood, and where no one recognized him, he became a shepherd as before.

He spent many nights weeping over himself, over his life spent so quickly; he wept over wealth, love, and knowledge, without realizing that this was the test of which the old oak Arra'ch had spoken to him; but after a long struggle in spirit with himself, he knew that there was a God other than in the books of the sages; and he prostrated himself within himself before this God, and at that moment the immense army of the spirits of the forest, of the Earth and of the Waters, came, preceded by the spirits of the Air, to pay him homage, to submit to his Spirit and to promise him obedience. Hans then said to them, "Do not submit to me, but to him whom I feel living in me, who has led my soul by secret ways, and who gives it at last Poverty, Goodness, and Life instead of Gold, Lust, and Science after which I have so long run."

This is the story of the blond little Hans, the foundling. I hope it has made you forget your sorrows a little, dear Stella.

ℒETTER VIII

THÉOPHANE TO STELLA

You cry, dear sister; you will still have joy, because *nothing exists without its opposite*; soon you will smile, soon you will have given up a little of yourself. You will never shed as many tears as you have made your brothers shed; know well that nature would have no hold on us if we did not give her some; we are attacked about as much as we have attacked before, whether eight days or a hundred centuries ago; the Justice of things has scrupulous accountants who do not omit the smallest of our incursions. Then why cry? you will say, "Ah!" Dear sister, cry not because of the pains you are suffering, but cry of repentant love and compassion; lose yourself, sink, rush headlong into a plunge to the abyss of humility and holocaust. Then you will taste the refreshing and serene flavor of peace; the beating of angelic wings will refresh your heart; you will sleep in the arms of the divine messengers and your spirit will be led to the sacred mountains against whose sides the oceans of astral forces and essences beat without wearing them down.

ꟓETTER IX

ANDRÉAS TO STELLA

Here I go again for the Orient, which is like my second homeland. I was consumed with curiosity about the strangers to whom I had to present my my credentials; I had been told about them: they are positivist scientists, experimenters; and the brain of a Westerner always refuses at first to admit that there can be experimenters somewhere else than in the laboratories of his country. Disembarked in a small port on the Malabar coast, I had orders to walk around the city, dressed as an Indian, with a certain amulet on my wrist; I scrupulously carried out these instructions and, towards evening, a lower-caste man came to me and took me out of the city; there I found a light carriage which transported us during the night up to the Ghats, whose ascent we made by foot. The escarpments of these mountains did not allow me to enjoy the freshness of the air, the calm of the night nor the serenity of the landscape; the brambles, the stones, some fear also of the wild beasts and the venomous vermin occupied all of my strength. After two hours of ascent, we arrived at a kind of granite plateau, stripped of grass, and on which were worked far and wide small heaps of stones, arranged in a circle; my guide led me towards the most considerable of these mounds, the center of which was a rocky mass rather similar to the standing stones of the Celtic countries; the blocks of stone formed an irregular vault under which we dragged ourselves on all fours. At the end was not a well but an irregular hole, into which my guide disappeared and where I followed him, while he guided with his hands my feet, groping along the irregular walls. We descended a few meters, and an inclined corridor brought us in half an hour to the center of an oubliette where reptiles were crawling among some human skulls. We were entering the ruins of one of those numerous Brahmanic cities that their population has abandoned, or that civil wars have destroyed; there are many of them in the Deccan, say the pandits. The access to the one where I was brought was wonderfully defended by the jungle and its population of gray monkeys, snakes, panthers, and tigers. The spectacle of a Hindu city in ruins invaded by the jungle is an admirable thing; it is the ideal of the fairy tale and the fantastic; the life of the inhabitants of the forest is different there too; it seems a little civilized, if one can say so: the birds sing there, the insects buzz there, the monkeys chatter there each one in turn and with some *savoir-vivre*; it is the roar of the tiger or the meow of the panther which is the leader of this living orchestra; the silences are majestic and full of secrecy, the ensembles deafening.

My guide was hurrying through the terraces with disjointed slabs, under the demolished colonnades and the crossroads full of wild grass; the immense sculpted roof of a pagoda darkened the sky suddenly above our heads; we had arrived. There, I was handed over to a

Vaishnavite brahmin, who greeted me in English and presented me with fruits and iced drinks. However I examined the structure of the temple which, for the beauty of its mass and the richness of its details, did not yield in anything to the most famous monuments of Benares and Ellora; as far as my memories of Tantras made me believe, this temple must have been built in the honor of Ganesha, the elephant god. It consisted of an immense enclosure or circular gallery, comprising five other smaller enclosures; two temples were erected high, the first one included three altars, with their mitre-shaped vaults; in the middle of the height extended an interior courtyard or ellipsoidal terrace, at the two focal points of which were set up the fourth and fifth altars. All the sculptures and friezes represented the legend of Shiva more or less as described in the Skanda Purana. Stone was the only material used in the decoration of this immense architecture.

Parama Shiva and his twenty-five *mourthis* are sculpted on the first of these pyramids; on the second, we see Daksha in the midst of the Pradjapatis, doing penance to Shiva; begetting the first thousand of his sons, the *Haryashva*s, then the second thousand, *Shabalashva*s, who govern the subtle essences of the Universe or *Tattwas*; then his sixty daughters, among whom shone Uma, the wife of Shiva; and the long doctrine of these characters, each one fulfilling the symbol of the cosmic force he expresses, unfolds on all the faces of the quadrangular altar, the pyramid and the columns.

The third altar shows the fall of Daksha and the transformation of his daughter Uma into Parvati on Mount Himavān; while Shiva, in the form of Dakshinamurthy (தட்சிணாமஊர்த்தி), the aspect of the Hindu god Shiva as the guru of all types of knowledge, tries in vain to initiate the *mounis* under the shade of a banyan tree, and then tries again on the summit of the Kailasa Temple; during this initiation, the *asuras* spread over the earth and commit a thousand atrocities; then the Mahadeva emanates Kumara or Subramanyia, the spiritual warrior.

The fourth altar recounts the incidents of the birth of the second of Shiva's sons, Ganesha the peaceful. The fifth altar, according to the myth of the Linga Purana (लिङ्गपुराण) represents the fivefold Shiva and his twenty sons in the guise of Sadyojāta, through whom life is absorbed, Vâmadeva, who fulfills the law and ritual, Tatpurusha, who fixes beings in the supreme science and essence, Aghora the terrible, who teaches Yoga, and finally Isâna the form of all forms, who fuses together Union, Reason, Penance, Science, Religious Observance, and the twenty-seven other qualities of the soul that has attained Deliverance.

Along the outer peristyle crawled the serpents of Eternity with their seven heads; the symbolic guardians of the mysteries stood from distance to distance; the sacred elephants, bearers of Gnosis and porters of the Temple, lowered their granite trunks and tusks towards the visitor; the support disappeared under the swarm of demonic forms, confined, according to the books, to the lower worlds of the Invisible; under the leaves of the cactus, euphorbia and banana trees, the puckered faces, the hanging canines of the vampires, the flesh-eating demons known as *Pishachas* in the Buddhist and Hindu mythology, where the Kataputanas and the Ulkamukha Pretas are modeled in the shadows; on the outer surfaces of the walls are sculpted the celestial concerts of the *Gandharvas*, dancing and playing their instruments; Towards the north are the images of Soma and Indra; towards the east those of the guardians of the treasures, the *Yakshas*, presided over by Kubera and Yakhshini his wife; on the west side is the army of the *Rakshasas* commanded by Khadga-Râvana who gives victory over the enemies.

The worship of all these more or less demonic entities is still in force, even among the upper classes, in Travancore and in Malabar. I have even witnessed a very strange occurrence in this locality, which my friend will remind me to tell her.

But I am lingering too long, I think, in dry descriptions; I have let a brahmin offer me refreshments and I resume my story at the point where I had interrupted it.

This brahmin, thin of body, with a large nose and beautiful eyes, although sunken in their sockets, explained to me in very pure English that everything in this old temple transformed into a laboratory was at my disposal, and that all his guests considered themselves, because of the high recommendation which had allowed me to penetrate there, as my servants. I thanked him in the interminable and hyperbolic formulas of oriental politeness, and began the tour of the property for me.

"There is one thing I would beg you to do, first of all," said my guide; "it is not to hurry, to consider that you have a lot of time ahead of you and that you are going to be confronted with complete novelties. Haste or impatience would therefore be obstacles and not help." I promised him that I would make efforts to realize the oriental calm, asking him to use a great deal of patience with me himself, and a series of wonders began for me. "This temple," my guide told me, "is of the laboratory and workshop class," so I was not to find rare minerals, precious essences, or devices of psychological magic; the scientists who inhabit it study more or less what we call the physical forces, and this by means of a small number of exquisitely sensitive devices; This sensitivity is obtained by the isolation of the magnetic currents which pass in the ground and those which circulate in the atmosphere; for this purpose, they employ special processes of manufacture of the metal wires; these processes are always manual; one rejects the use of the machines, the rolling mills and other industrial improvements; all is done there by hand, and with a patience which would weary the most patient of our saints of the West. To give you an idea, Stella, I saw a worthy Hindu, sitting in the shadow of the first floor, tapping a copper wire with a hammer that weighed well over twenty grams; I could hear the mechanical noise of his blows from three o'clock in the morning until sunset; then another striker came to replace him during the night, and this work lasted, I was told, for months.

I will spare you the description of all the devices my guide – his name was Sankhyananda – used to dismantle and reassemble with dexterity, for the convenience of the explanations. There is one, however, whose use is so extraordinary and seems a story likely to be written by Jules Verne, that I want to tell you about it in detail to amuse your imagination.

But I realize that my letter is already quite long: I have not spoken to you, – nor of myself for that matter. Forgive me in consideration of what zeal I have put into fulfilling my role as narrator. See you soon, my dear memory, still so alive in me.

ℒETTER X

THÉOPHANE TO STELLA

L ong ago, longer than you yourself suppose, dear child, things have been conspiring around you to induce you to listen to the bewitching whispers of Eros-King. Many ears are open within us to listen to him, and our naivety is so great, little children who believe that they are men, that we imagine we are all in the little corner of ourselves where he speaks. Our "I" is infinitely higher and more vast, but we call "I" precisely that through which we touch the Void, and we ignore the radiant essences through which we reach the Absolute.

You thought you loved because of a nervous sympathy, or because you had experienced similar emotions, or out of kindness, or out of weariness, or out of curiosity, or perhaps because the sun was too hot, or there was electricity in the air; and you always said to yourself, "I have loved such and such a being"; this is not true, however; it is not you who have performed these acts, it is soldiers of yourself, often undisciplined, but who have at least the excellent habit of going forward and making the secret Stella, who is hardly courageous and recoils from the effort, experiment.

𝒬ETTER XI

ANDRÉAS TO STELLA

I made you wait a long time for the continuation of my visit to the lost city; that which I found here is what exercised my curiosity: books, apparatuses, and experiments. I threw myself into it, it is necessary to confess it to you with some shame, hoping to deaden my pain and to forget you a little; I almost succeeded there; science is a jealous mistress and one who does not suffer even a wandering thought in her lovers. Also, for the moment, she is parsimonious and does not fill me with her favors.

But I want to resume my story; I had promised you the description of a fantastic machine: you will judge for yourself if my astonishment was justified.

Through this crowd of devices and working instruments, Sankhyananda stopped in front of a kind of cubic box made of a substance as yellow as gold and transparent as glass. "This," he said, "is a *Duracâpàlam*, what you might call in your language a telemobile. We use this to travel to the planets of our material universe." I opened my eyes very widely, but my interlocutor continued, "This is still an application of the *tattwa* theory, part of which your monistic philosophers have rediscovered with the fourth dimension. Here is the sequence of reasoning that led us to this application."

Here my interlocutor gave me the known theory of the Hindu rationalist system on the constituent elements of the Universe; a long and tedious theory which I will not transcribe, since it is not absolutely necessary for the understanding of the system.

"All external objects are perceived by one of the five senses, and as each of these senses vibrates synchronously with only one of the forms of the universal substance, the objects of external perception can be classified according to the five elements which we call *Tattwas* and whose nature and properties I have explained to you. That of the æther is to be perceived by the sense of hearing; that of air, fire, water, and earth are to be perceived respectively by touch, sight, taste, and smell. Thus these objective mental manifestations caused by these various sensations possess the same specific qualities as the external objects that cause them. They also have certain generic qualities. For example, sound has a form. The notes, the various tones, are as fixed on their plane as solid substances are on the earthly plane; technically, the soniferous minima is as cohesive a mass as the atomic block of visible matter; each acoustic form possesses in the mind an unchanging existence.

Sound appears to us, as we conceive it, to be endowed with a certain softness. This softness, which we call *Sneha*, is the quality which gives the molecules of a substance the power to slide easily over each other; and indeed, everyone knows that sounds flow more or less, are more or less fluid.

Moreover, sound has its own temperature; the acoustic mental impression often becomes a determinant of heat: the heating or cooling effects of music are well known.

Lastly, sound has a force of impulse or locomotion (*pranâmitva*); it determines movements, and the mind that hears warlike or dancing music soon knows this faculty.

Thus the æther, our *Akash*à, has a specific quality, sound, and generic qualities: form, fluidity, caloric, movement.

Now, there are classes of sounds, some of which contain more perfect forms, some of which give off more heat, and some of which contain considerable quantities of movement; we know these classes; we know how to emit these sounds; we even know how to strengthen them by increasing the rigidity of the sounding board which brings them to consciousness, I mean by bringing the tension of the mind to a high degree. So here is an acquired point; we possess a *mantram* which, pronounced under certain conditions of nervous electricity, is capable of setting in motion a certain quantity of matter, that is to say, of subtracting it from the action of terrestrial gravity.

Let us pass to another obscure point.

The conception of space is one of the most difficult to imagine. You Europeans conceive only the physical, material space; it is that one that you call the real space; for us, it is simply the illusory one, while the real one is the one that some of your philosophers begin to discover. Physical space cannot be infinite; this is a truth both of tradition and of reasoning, which I hope to be able to make you feel, moreover, by experience. To suppose physical space to be infinite would be to suppose an infinite number (its measure) to be realized, which is not admitted.

If this space is finite, it has a shape, and this shape is spherical, because there is no reason for it to extend in one direction rather than another. What is the function of space? It is to be the locus of all creatures; therefore, space is the passive while the principle of creatures, God, if you will, is the active. And here you recognize one of the symbolic meanings of the myths of all religions: Brahman and Maya, the Word and the Virgin, Purusha and Prakriti.

In this immense though finite space, whose real dimensions we know by special means of investigation, bathe all beings, formed of all the matters of which science knows only a part. Now, these beings, which are each like a kind of matter, are all born, live, and die, since by definition, they are creatures. With these two points in mind, let us return to our telemobile, and seek what qualities such a machine must have in order to be able to transport itself and subsist in all points of space.

These qualities are two: the inalterability of its materials and the energy of a force independent of all forces: cosmic, that is to say, superior to them. It is understood that we always remain in the plane of the visible universe, the only one that exists for our compatriots.

These conditions seem, at first sight, impossible to fulfill; however, here is how these difficulties were solved. It is possible for the chemists of our temples, whom you may call alchemists, to produce materials that cannot be attacked by the physical agents of our planet: atmosphere, water, heat, light, electricity, magnetism, ethereal forces, etc.; but in order to produce materials that cannot be attacked by the destructive agents of another planet, they would have to know these agents, which would be tantamount to knowing the planet that we are trying to explore.

Our observations of the stars, not only of their mechanics but also of their biology, what you call astronomy and astrology, observations preserved for some twenty thousand years, have enabled us to draw up for each planet a table of probabilities of its physical constitution and of the qualities of the universal Life of which it is the support. Each of the brahminic observatories establishes every night a series of reports, which are then centralized, compared, and classified; so that the chances of error of our probabilities are reduced to a very small fraction. A machine, therefore, which would carry an observer in space at the greatest possible distance from the earth and in the direction of the nearest planet, could be used to verify the accuracy of our astronomical observations and, provided with this certain information, our chemists could build a second machine capable of remaining alternately on the earth and on the moon.

The ancient and venerable Magic which, every century, wants to manifest its presence in your Europe, to gather the suffrages of some elite minds together with the calumnies of the crowd, and its vile enthusiasms, more humiliating than the calumnies, is not a science of metaphysics and hollow dreams; it is an exact and positive science; the real magicians are not exalted, but engineers and mechanics. The naive people who hypnotize themselves in front of pentacles and *yantrams* do not know that these drawings are the blueprints of a special kinematics and whose domains are those mysterious spaces with four, five, six, and seven dimensions, the very idea of which seems to your philosophers a pure madness. There are, however, brains that are active in these spaces, that live, work, and make machines and works of art in them: the pentacles are the lines of force of these machines, the framework of these invisible but active statues, of these inaudible but fertile symphonies for noble hearts and truly human souls.

That you consider, with Descartes, all matter as extent and all extent as matter; that is to say, full, absolute space; or matter as extended and impenetrable with interposed voids; or whether you admit the famous system of pre-established harmony; or its modification, which endows the monads with external activities and gives them attractive and repulsive forces, none of these four opinions will prevent you from rallying to ours. And the more you advance in knowledge, the more you will see that the traditional doctrines are sufficient, by their very presence, to clear up the disputes which arise in the closed field of philosophical esotericism.

Yes, extent is substantial; yes, the simple forces that fertilize it really exist.

To seize one and the other, such is the double problem that the telemotor seems to solve.

We have already discovered one of these forces in the dynamic property of the acoustic æther, which is eroded under certain conditions. It is necessary to find the point of support of this force, a material center where it can be stored, and finally devices to direct it.

If we consider the simple elements of matter, the æther atoms, by definition, these simple elements cannot have any action on each other since they do not touch each other, for if they did touch each other, they would do so by their entire surface. We must therefore imagine a subtler fluid in which the æther atoms swim like fish in water; this fluid would be formed of atoms infinitely smaller than the æther atoms; these atoms, animated by vertiginous velocities, constantly shock the æther atoms and serve them as intermediary for the propagation of the vibratory movements. Here, the scientific hypothesis, supported by the differential calculation, is verified by numerous experiments made by means of optical devices, much more powerful than your telescopes and your microscopes, and of which what the popular superstition calls the magic mirrors are a rudimentary and remote sketch.

It has been remarked that man reproduces in his machines and utensils the models provided to him by Nature. Let us continue our study of the matter, and see how it will organize itself; perhaps we will find, lurking between two small atoms, the idea which we miss to realize our machine.

Our scientists have calculated the atomic volumes of your so-called simple bodies, and in spite of all the uncertainty of these calculations, since no one knows the real volume of an atom, we can notice that the atomic volumes of bodies of the same family are in simple ratios: I dispense with quoting M. Dumas and M. Würtz to prove this. If, therefore, a fortunate chance places in the hands of the chemist an agent capable of modifying the positions of the chemical atoms in a body, one conceives the possibility of transmuting chlorine into iodine, or carbon into rubidium.

The subtle fluid of which I have just indicated the probability of existence has been known experimentally to our sages for centuries; it is the *Vyoma-Pantchaka Akasha*, whose fivefold nature you will find described in the Mandala Brahmana. One of these natures, the fourth, the *Surya Akasha*, is especially qualified for accumulation and storage; the study of its properties has enabled us to choose the material accumulator, each of whose molecules can serve as a carrier for an enormous quantity of those spirit molecules which belong to the fourth dimension. This accumulator is a kind of crystal book: you know that crystal is a sublimated and perfect product of what your hermeticists call old Saturn; the lamellae are cut in a shape reminiscent of catacoustic surfaces. When it comes to loading it, one of our *Sannyâsis* trains himself in advance, and, having reached the necessary state of tension, he repeats the secret mantra on the apparatus, ten thousand times, a hundred thousand times if necessary, until, from the depths of the crypts where the apparatus has been lowered for this operation, the shrill vibration of the crystal lamellae can be heard on the surface of the ground.

It was necessary to find a framework where to place the explorer so as to protect him against the attacks of the environment: changes of temperature, electric discharges, incursions of unknown beings, etc. Here is how we have established the terms of the problem.

Let us take up here the theories of pangeometry, or hyperbolic geometry, which German and Russian scientists have invented in recent years. Whether we stick to Euclid's system or to János Bolyai, the geometry of the sphere is identical; here are the theoretical results that we need to know: in the new geometry, the circumference no longer tends towards the straight line as its radius increases, but towards a limiting curve distinct from the straight line while remaining tangent to it; this is the horocycle. This curve parallel to a straight line generates surfaces and volumes that naturally develop inside Euclidean surfaces and volumes. It is these volumes generated by the horocycle that we have managed to realize inside a three-dimensional material body.

This body we have chosen, is made of a material that is unassailable by all known physical agents; it is a precious metal whose molecular constitution has been profoundly altered by a special beating and very slow cooking processes. This yellow and translucent box that you see before you was once gold. As such it could only condense the luminous æther, one of the forms of our Vedic Agni. The preparations we have made it undergo have made it suitable for penetration by that *Surya Akasha* of which I spoke earlier.

Don't touch it," said the brahmin, at a gesture I made, "you will find yourself very uncomfortable. The experimenter who wants to use this device must first have trained his physical body in such a way that it can safely withstand electric shocks which would strike down an ordinary man. It is simply a special yoga to be performed. We have no trained subjects in the temple at present, and besides, the atmospheric electricity at this time of year is not conducive to this experiment, but if you are still with us next year you can see and judge."

But enough science like that; I will tell you the rest another time, my Mona Lisa, and let us speak now a little about you, who remain, you know it well, my dearest concern.

You complain about losing your fortune; this is a natural and foreseen event; our soul cannot possess the whole universe, whatever the metaphysicians say; when it thinks it does, it is only a cloudy reverie; to possess treasures is not to imagine what one would do with hypothetical tons of gold locked up in vaults in Spain, if I may say so; it is to be able to take this gold with one's hands and to throw it where one pleases. But gold is one thing and the inner light is another; and unfortunately they have no affinity with each other.

Gold is the measure, the bushel with which one can buy ideas, lands, precious materials, enjoyments; it is, in a word, the sign of property; light, on the other hand, whose essence is universality, denies itself to those who separate themselves from the world by becoming owners. This is why the old mystical dreamers called gold an infernal form and put it under the government of one of the first captains of Satanas, Mammon.

We are so childish that, when we have been given the chance to catch the butterfly we have been chasing for a few months, we imagine ourselves to be the masters of the butterfly; it is the little insect which, however, has put us out of breath and which escapes us dead as soon as we hold it. We put beautiful phrases around these games of kids; we call it love, ambition, the desire for glory; we even raise these hyperboles to the height of a flashy lie that we take for ourselves first. Thus there are famous men, heroes "who died for their country"; others "who created a race", who have never known any other feeling than the pride of possession and the desire of enjoyment.

However, it is true that man is the king of nature; but he is this king by his soul, by his essential and divine principle, not by the small instruments of work that we lend ourselves and that we call intelligence, talent, skill, genius, etc. He takes these instruments for himself and, looking at Nature – his patrimony – he says to himself: How am I going to make sure that she does not escape me? But Nature knows where this brain, these muscles, this ingenuity come from; she remembers having lent them to the soul of man so that this one can use the forces of that one; but now her children are thrown against their mother to reduce her to slavery; the mother defends herself, without correcting the kids too hard; and now the man who breaks his nails against the obstacles cries, screams, takes the sky as witness, while he is himself the craftsman of his own disappointments. Ah, how ridiculous we would be if we were not worthy of pity. That is why the owners of money, honor, are in reality miserable slaves. The one who renounces all things keeps them at his disposal, or rather,] Nature presents him, as if to her true overlord, with the keys to her secret palaces. Now, when the true light descends into the soul, it gently corrects its attitude, and, making it look at itself, shows it its real position in front of the vast world. The ancient error then falls from the eyes, and we begin to understand what I have just explained to you too confusedly for my liking. Every bit of this gold that leaves you is one of your old chains that breaks; a passion, that is to say a passivity, goes away that your soul replaces by a spiritual energy that goes after the essential vigor of the beings of which you had until then possessed only the mortal envelope.

A little courage, then, dear friend; a little more courage, for many are the chains we have forged for ourselves, and many are the excuses our laziness finds to make us wear them a little longer.

ℚETTER XII

THÉOPHANE TO STELLA

All humanity weeps, dear child; and the higher the creature, the finer its sensitivity, the more it increases its power of suffering. There as everywhere, what is secret is more active and more acute than what is manifest; the great sorrows are hidden from the eyes of the world; they live in sumptuous palaces, with magnificent facades, statues, and decorations; but they are found in dark recesses known only to familiars; they torture in silence and in solitude those who are called the great, the fortunate, and the powerful; where have you ever seen more tragic masks if not among the triumphants of ambition and lucre and glory? Every famous man carries with him the mythical vulture that rips his chest, but none wants to admit it, and they would all die of pride sooner than humble themselves.

This pride, however, is necessary because it is a powerful explosive. Remember that what is true in the worlds of matter is also true in the worlds of spirit; the harder the rock, the more hold the dynamite has on it; thus, the firmer the soul, the more the feelings which animate it give it constancy, strength, and energy. This is why the great conductors of souls all recommend to their disciples to keep their feelings secret, to act without revealing the motives of their acts, to suffer and enjoy in silence. Aren't immutability and impassibility the aesthetic signs of the Absolute?

However, if we are strong, we are also weak little children; the big pompous words, with which we exalt ourselves until we have agreed to call heroism, are a little like the sword, the little cap and the tin cuirass by means of which each toddler imagines himself prancing at the head of an invincible regiment. In all men, with very rare exceptions, there is ambition, or avarice, or love, or hatred, or vanity: four-penny trumpets, at the sounds of which we intoxicate ourselves with complacency and conviction.

But for us to measure the emptiness of a thing, we must have had it all to ourselves; each of us must know all these efforts, these disappointments, these anguishes, these triumphs, these pangs, these transports, these rages, these intoxications before even the conception of universal serenity, of great compassion, is possible for him. What the Law asks of us is to live as intensely, as deeply as our physical, moral, and intellectual strength allows. Life has no other goal than itself; it is she who pushes us in the laces of desire; it is her eternal force which is reflected in all the little particular existences; and it is she whom we persist in not recognizing, closing our eyes to her rays, blocking our ears to her great initiating voice; or at least wanting to hear it only through these imperfect instruments, marked by the seal of destruction and death, which are our intelligence and our animism.

But then, will you say, men are an unconscious herd that strays at random from its whims and that no pastor directs us towards good pastures? No, we have guides, and many; but, different in this from the shepherds of the earth, they take care only of those who come to them and leave us free to follow them or to live as we please; the sheep see their shepherd, but they do not know the master of the farm whom the shepherd obeys; so we can know our pastors and speak to them, but the masters of our guardians are hidden from us; they live elsewhere, in the city, where they work with more depth and generality; their sphere is beyond our conception; we cannot understand them, but only, from time to time, recognize their invisible presence by some unexpected pleasure, some relief from our work.

When, therefore, we have strained all the fibers of our psychic energies to the point of breaking them, when the reactions which our carelessness provoked on the part of Nature become too strong for us to resist, we begin to suspect that man will become - that man may become the king of creation, but that he is not yet; we had climbed up to then along the slopes of the mountain of Self; we will go down the steep slopes; we go from pride to humility, from glory to obscurity, from wealth to poverty. God has therefore conquered man; the creature perceives the true path, and his heart will feel with joy all the pains of this mystical agony, by which he is given to die to himself in order to be reborn later in the eternal Light and in the Bliss of the Spirit.

This is the future that awaits us all; such is the path by which your soul, dear penitent, will be led; many solicitudes have, from now on, their eyes open on you; you will never be alone, no more than any other soul. The Eternal is alone, but all creatures have relatives and friends.

ꟼETTER XIII

ANDRÉAS TO STELLA

few words to tell you a story, dear Stella. There was with us on one excursion one of those professional snake charmers called *saperas*; he was a silent old man called Hamira Bhangorr; born in Bahowal, in Hoshiarpur, he had prowled a bit everywhere and rendered quite a few services, said the *Sais*, to Nana-Sahib.

He saw a cobra bite our *mahout*; immediately rushing on the serpent, he presented it with a piece of dark red resin, oval, which he constantly carried with him; the reptile fled in the tall grass; Hamira first applied his resin to the wound, which was already black, then a piece of dry root and, in a few minutes, the swelling disappeared, a few drops of blood beaded on the skin, and the *mahout* was able to resume walking. Hamira turned to me to explain that its resin was the solidified slime of the Markhor, the snake-killing deer, and the root was that of the plant which the Markhor uses as a counter-poison. I knew from experience that you should never smile at a person if you don't want to lose your confidence forever; I listened to his story seriously.

ꝒETTER XIV

THÉOPHANE TO STELLA

Heart and intelligence: the former is love, the latter is science; and let me here, dear sorrowful one, tell you one of my favorite daydreams. You know that the most cherished, among all these imaginations in which you must have been told that I delight, is the idea that all that exists lives; but not of that collective and mute life which scientists attribute to their forces and their atomic combinations, *but of a real, objective, concrete, free and responsible existence.*

All that is tangible on our earth, the natural objects, the inventions of man, the ideas of philosophers, the legislating wills of kings, the needs of the crowd, the humblest bits of matter that we have softened for our convenience, all of these are living, individual beings like you and me; like us too, they have something visible, sensitive, and something invisible; as with us again, it is their invisibility where their strength is hidden. The very characters that my pen traces on this paper have a spirit that vivifies them.

But here, let's not fall into an idolatrous fetishism. This vivifying spirit has energy only so much as I, scribe, trainer of its body, infuse it with my thought, and that the purity of my thought or my intention is able to attract the eternal type of Life that blazes somewhere beyond the worlds. These characters will only enjoy a temporary life; if you tear up my letter, they will become an anarchic tribe of little savages; if you burn it, they will die to physical life and then be reborn into another form of existence.

What I have just said to you, probably in a confused way, is also true of the words: An idiom is, to redevelop formulas dear to M. de la Palisse, an idiom, not only of languages spoken on this earth, but also of all the languages spoken in all the planets, where beings possessing the gift of speech can live: so, if you do not find the leap too great, a word is a microscopic image of the universal Life, or better, of one of the beings that contain it.

Do you feel now that if I write or if I pronounce the words: four, thought, good, etc., I draw, with a pen or with my voice, a small photograph, deformed, of a being: the Four, Thought, Good, etc. who raises his gigantic stature on the summit of an unknown mountain or who walks on the ethereal waves of some cosmic river? It may be a hundred meters from the surface of the earth, or beyond Sirius; for matter is penetrable; there are more than three dimensions in space; what do we know?

And if the civilized Stella is frightened by these paradoxes, let her listen a little to the savage Stella who knows well that the soul of man is always attached to the absolute truth, and that, as a result of this union, more intimate than philosophers and priests imagine, man cannot beget something totally false.

Thus this admirable symbolism of nature, this free vegetation, produced by the marriage of the efforts of human reason and the help of divine goodness, causes the profound truths to be hidden in commonplace language.

We use the word "love" or the word "reason" a thousand times a day. Who wonders why the first is of the masculine gender, the second of the feminine gender? Why does one express the charm of your sisters, Stella, and the other the strength of my brothers?

I spoke to you about sacrifices the other day; here is the second to do: forget the books, they are not made for you; immerse yourself in maternal and fruitful life; listen with your heart to the beating of his heart. Let scholars enumerate the forms of matter, the armies of the stars, the legions of plants; leave their instruments and their algebras; your mathematics must be the rays of the God who is in you; your microscopes are the efforts of your charity, always on the alert. Service is your motto.

ℒETTER XV

ANDRÉAS TO STELLA

Y ou are in the hand of Théophane, friend whom I am beginning to love again with a new tenderness; I warned you. Now that you have set foot on the road, you must follow it to the end; such is, at least, the law according to my terrible Orientals. I myself am in a similar position; my whole intellectual edifice is collapsing, and I have to walk, impassive, without glancing back, without bidding farewell to all these thoughts, painfully conquered since my adolescence.

These brahmins have a depth of character, a determination, an absolutism in the act that frightens us, we French dilettantes. They are no longer men, they are forces of Nature. The empire they have over themselves has something, in my opinion, extra-human; one would say that their soul has undergone something like a transplant, or rather that it has been grafted onto some essence coming from an impassive and higher ground. Good fathers, good sons, good husbands, good patriots, where they disconcert me is in the strength they deploy in the midst of the struggles of thought and the mysterious combats sustained against unknown forces, more indomitable than the wild ass of Turkestan. Remind me, in this connection, of a second story that I must tell you about one day when they will give me some respite. These painful phases when the psychic being seems to disintegrate like a field that one turns over to be sown again, they say are useful and necessary, and I begin to believe with them that, in the soul, as on earth, no flowers grow without the seed having died before. Poor consolations, you will say; Alas! I am not an enchanter and, separated from you by thousands of leagues, space remains a barrier for me; it will fall one day, my Masters tell me, I hope with all my heart that Théophane will also make it fall for you. Forgive me for leaving you so quickly; I have to go back to the laboratory, if one can call with such a word that evokes the cold rooms decorated with cupboards of the universities of Europe, a courtyard where the stones disappear under the pressure of the vines, where the air is saturated with aromas, where the moon replaces the electric lamps, where masters and pupils are dressed in white robes instead of frock coats, and lastly where the lessons are said in verse. This is another thing that would make the professors of the College of France jump if they suspected it. To teach physics and chemistry in rhythmic sentences! To claim to unite beauty and accuracy, poetic spirit and experimental rigor! This is, however, thanks to the admirable instrument that Sanskrit has become handled in the oriental style and no longer Bopp or Max Muller.

But to tell you all that would take a very long time; and then, I promised discretion on many things and the men with whom I live are discreet of an unheard-of kind; one would say that they learned an art of forgetting, as we invent mnemonic systems in the West. What new things to tell you!

See you soon, oh you who may one day be my good Genius.

ꟴETTER XVI

THÉOPHANE TO STELLA

Allow me to call you my child. The day is not far off when I will be able to do something for you that will somewhat excuse the protectiveness of this title, for we are all children of the same Father, and we are all worth as much in His eyes. My child, as I was saying, I had begun to speak to you about Love, and its inescapable spouse, Death, came immediately to visit you. For this sadness, this discouragement, these doubts, despair, dismal indifference to everything, these are the forms of one of the most painful deaths given to humans to endure. I say "given", because these sufferings are beneficial and saving; I won't tell you why or how you're going to live and then you'll understand everything. Your friend, Andréas, had a recipe that would have helped you bear these tortures; he did not tell you, not only because he had been ordered to remain silent, but above all because he did not believe that you were capable of putting it into practice.

Here is the recipe: it essentially consists in discovering in the depths of our consciousness the pedestal where our true self is enthroned, in climbing this pedestal and watching from there our soldiers fight: the thought that crumbles, the heart that loses its enthusiasm, the will abandoned by faith. But this recipe is dangerous, because we thus come to no longer be interested in Life, and we sin seriously every time we neglect to act. We are soldiers and laborers; our duty is to fight against the darkness, and after defeating it, to clear the deserts it inhabited. Books are work tools, science is not an end, but a means.

Your woman's heart makes you feel all these things; you don't have to stop there. You love Andréas, your love is a living angel: send it to him; it does not know the distances; the Spirit is everywhere at once; you will have to support the exile, to guide him perhaps, at least to intercede for him. You will thus know, by experience, what an invincible sword is Love, why and how it is active, why science is passive and what essences are nourished by perfect men. Such is the Great Work that will be given to you to accomplish, you two.

Already now, are you not secretly warned by light touches within yourselves of what happens, happy or harmful, to your beloved? Love grows insofar as it gives itself. So love all those around you, and you will love all the more deeply the one with whom you will one day be one soul.

142

ꝒETTER XVII

ANDRÉAS TO STELLA

While vegetable juices are slowly cooking in a copper basin, I will be able, while watching the fire, to pay off the first part of my debt. You remember that I promised you the story of a ceremony of modern Shivaism; if I was able to attend despite being European, it is thanks to my knowledge of the customs and the language of the country, and also because the sun has made my skin something similar to the epidermis of a yogi; moreover, my friends from the Ganesha pagoda had accompanied me. This happened a few months after my arrival in the country.

First of all, I must tell you that in most towns in Malabar, religion is twofold; there is the one that we follow officially, in broad daylight, then the other that we deal with in the shadows, at night; the first is nothing more than a series of complicated rites. The second, clearly bad, wins its adherents by something which resembles all that is said of the ancient sorcerer's sabbaths. And Hindus, whatever their caste, the majority of their priests, as little instructed in the mysteries of the Sudras as the last, find themselves, on certain nights, in the jungle, pell-mell, all distinctions confused, the rich, the poor, the warrior, the actor, the wrestler, the servant, carried away by the same frenzy, in a formidable hysterical whirlwind.

The place of the meeting was a vast rocky plateau, upon which the care of the priests and the sect had, over a fairly large space, cleared the ground of the thorny shrubs which covered it everywhere else, for the lands where brambles grow are very pleasant to Shiva. There are there, for the only temple, a kind of platform of stones, on which stood a pyre, prepared in advance, and at the corners classic *lingams*. The ceremony included a feast and a religious ceremony. The feast, prepared by a few of the faithful established on the edge of the surrounding jungle, was distinguished by a Pantagruellian abundance and by the systematic violation of all the rules that the gods gave to men to know the permitted or forbidden foods. Game, illicit meat, alcoholic liquors, mulled wines, spicy roots: nothing was spared to ignite in the blood of the guests a fire which, in my opinion, contributed much to the religious part of the feast.

Unlike what usually takes place in the Shaktist meetings, there were no women in our assembly, but the fact of being among men did not take away from the assistants that gravity, so often imposing, under which the Hindu hides all his emotions; the very intoxication in which many fell was dignified and sober. I know only of lords who can bear so much alcohol with the same self-possession. My guides and I cautiously abstained from the feast; otherwise it would have been almost impossible to resist the dizziness of which the whole assembly would become prey.

After the feast, the assistants, under the direction

of some chiefs, began a slow and complicated dance whose figures symbolized, it seemed, the legend of Durga. During this time, a few veenas, tambourines, and a kind of clarinet supported in minor a psalmody sung, or rather murmured, by nine priests. This was where the weird side of the meeting began.

As these dances went on, vapors seemed to rise from the ground, which was, however, parched by the sun; they condensed, visible under the rays of the moon, in the center of each ring of dancers; then sandalwood, sprinkled with a fetid and sinister oil, was lit on the bonfire; various powders were thrown into the fire, melted butter, and bones which seemed to me to come from children, and the assistants united in such a way as to form a moving circle all around this improvised altar; the clouds which I had seen came to the sides of the hearth, and as a dancer fell in exaltation to the ground, a form like a woman detached itself from this white vapor, approached the one who was in the magnetic crisis, and little by little little by little the whole plateau became the scene of an orgy of lust next to which the Satyricon and Louise Sigée and the drawings of Jules Romain paled. The phenomenon was certainly objective, because, I repeat, as soon as I advanced a few steps towards the center of the stage, I felt magnetic currents of irresistible power seize me in the cerebellum.

Isn't it curious to find everywhere the same rites when man wants to deify the power of physical creation that Nature lends him?

Tomorrow, I think I have time to pay off my

second debt. May the Devas watch over your nights, dear abandoned one; think sometimes of the one who perhaps thinks too often of you.

Today I want to finish the story of the telemobile by giving you new details; I would ask you, so as not to repeat boring explanations, to refer to the beginning of my "scientific" report.

I told you that the brahmins consider the sonic fluid to be the highest telluric fluid, and how they establish a close relationship between its vibrations and those of thought. If therefore it is possible to invent a metal which is a good conductor of sound to a very high degree, we will build armatures of it which man, or rather the force of a specially trained brain, can load at will. We will therefore have a source of energy superior to all terrestrial dynamisms.

My Masters, or rather their ancestors, found this metal. Its manufacture requires infinite care; the material they use is an ore of aluminum. My information will stop there. Still, in that transparent case I told you about is the crystal accumulator. When it has to be charged, seven priests first submit to rigorous training for forty days. They only eat once a day, a kind of fish-meat porridge; the cell where they live is painted mauve and the walls are decorated with drawings representing the various variations of the force which it is to capture. They spend their time in a state analogous to hypnosis, obtained by the repetition of a word: the *mantram* of sound. The periods of these sessions are determined beforehand by a careful study of the magneto-telluric movements. Six of these priests charge the machine by the laying on of hands for seven days, during which they observe a rigorous fast. The seventh, which is the experimenter, remains in the cell and only enters the metal cage after loading [after the charging]. These men then offer a fantastic appearance. They can only go out at night, because the sun's rays burn their skin. Their complexion has become like ivory; their enlarged eyes shine with an unbearable brilliance. All their movements are counted; they save the least expense of strength.

Finally, on the seventh night, as soon as the sun has disappeared, the machine is transported to the cell where the training sessions take place; the six auxiliaries sit along the walls; the seventh enters the box whose translucent wall allows you to see its final preparations. He is naked, his whole body is coated with a special varnish which closes the openings; an insulating frame allows him to extend along the diagonal plane of the device; under his back are the accumulators; before his eyes is a disc of burnished gold; within reach of his hands rock crystal handles control the power sockets. His feet sink into two little boxes filled with black dust which is charcoal made from the wood of a kind of laurel tree. It must be remembered that the operator can no longer breathe as soon as he enters the device; he can, however, perform voluntary movements, since he alone turns the crystal levers. All this is done in silence; the assistants, lips and eyes closed, seem like statues. They had arranged for me, so that I could watch without danger, a small adjacent cell with a pane of violet glass. The experimental room is, it seems, untenable for anyone who has not undergone the required training; the fluidic waves condensed there can seriously affect the cerebrospinal nerves.

In five minutes, therefore, I saw these seven men making their preparations; we were buried a hundred meters underground, in the most absolute silence. I saw the operator's hands lower two levers, as our drivers do in the West to change gears; a piercing whistle pierced my temples, and the transparent gold crate with its engineer suddenly disappeared. I couldn't believe my eyes; I was awake, conscious, without fever, without excitement; I had taken in the morning only a little honey collected with my own hands; I was not hallucinating. So, there had been what spiritualists call a disintegration. I remained there for several hours without the six living statues having moved. Sankhyananda came to fetch me, promising to bring me back when the strange traveler returned. As I explained my doubts to him, he assured me that there had indeed been disintegration. "The metal of this mysterious device," he told me, "is so intimately saturated with sonic fluid that its image, its invisible frame, persists in the cell; the same is true for the body of the operator. Every day, your thoughts wander to China, to France, to the moon, but these journeys are real, you emit little travelers, invisible to your physical eyes, and who return to their starting point, which is, for you, the place where your physical self rests. But for us, our self is where our will is. If I think of Paris, I am really in Paris. Therefore, it is possible for me to also transport its physical envelope there, on condition that I leave here a nucleus where it can be rebuilt; this is what takes place in the room under our feet. Did you notice that a geometric figure was drawn on the ground where the accumulators were? This is the core of the reconstruction of the machine and the traveler.

I then found all this absurd and crazy. At the moment, these ideas seem very simple to me. Do not conclude, dear beloved, that it is I who have gone mad.

A few days later, Sankhyananda came to take me and escorted me back to the small glass cabinet. I found the six helpers in the same position. At a certain moment, a fluorescence crossed the semi-darkness; then the six stretched out their hands towards the little design engraved on the floor; a vapor floated then invaded almost all the room, and without any noise, the box of gold and the extended mummy were there again. The assistants took the operator, transported him at a run to another cellar, where they immersed him entirely, several times, in a hot bath which melted the varnish; he was rubbed and massaged; they gave him some food, and he went back up to the open air, as if he were not the hero of the most fantastic odyssey a poet could conceive.

The assistants had, meanwhile, put everything in order, closed the exits and reinstalled the *Duracâpàlam* in the laboratory; they spent the rest of the day minutely inspecting the walls of the cell, to fill in the slightest cracks.

How great is the intelligence of man, my dear Stella! And these prodigious scientists readily admit that they do not even know the entire alphabet of total

Science! These confessions should discourage me: they only give me more enthusiasm for work.

LETTER XVIII

THÉOPHANE TO STELLA

The news Andréas sends you is a test for you, my child, in the sense that the marvelous things he tells you could make you want to eat forbidden fruit, as Moses said. You have already understood that this forbidden fruit is not the science of life, but the science of intelligence. It is not without reason that Lucifer is the first of the scholars; he does indeed carry a light, but it is frozen by pride, it dies of the voluptuousness of being alone. The unknown type of scientist, the one whose dream (fortunately without being able to realize it), by all men intoxicated by the force of their thought, is this fallen archangel, created for Life and to whom his pride makes him prefer the image of Life; because in the latter he reigns, while in the former he should serve.

All men go through the same ordeal at some point; the one you love is not far from crossing this formidable turning point. Ah! May the forces of your love be exalted to move the angels who protect it. Make friends, lots of friends, so that you find auxiliaries at the time of battle. Amass a treasure that you can easily draw from in a while.

You know that you can do nothing if Nature does not lend you thousands of servants; What combinations, rivalries, and protections are needed for you to cross a crossroads without being knocked down by a horse. None of your acts is therefore indifferent, and since the will which directs them is the same which, in the course of previous centuries, has always plunged you more and more deeply into the mirages of the Self, of Egoism, in the false splendors of the Black Light, learn little-by-little to replace this will with the wish of the beings around you. Try to do the will of others, you will quickly manage to do the will of the Father; and when you get there, your acts will be alive in eternity, because they will be accomplished by the Word, the only son of God.

Feel, dear child, how true these things are. Doesn't your heart beat faster reading teachings that aren't mine, besides? I send them to you as they were sent to me. The fidelity with which you in turn publish them will therefore be the measure by which you will feel your nothingness, where you will burn with the inexpressible fire of divine Love.

May your life be an uninterrupted prayer.

ꞯETTER XIX

ANDRÉAS TO STELLA

I t is today, beloved, that I finish my last fantastic tale. It is true, however, and the impression I felt while living it was so deep that many ideas matured in me, and the possibility of a synthesis finally appeared to me. But let's not do too much metaphysics; let's content ourselves with transcendent physics.

My masters believe that the physico-chemical forces which they study are not scattered here and there in the vast domain of biological facts; they believe that there are on the earth larger analogues of what our physicists call an electric field, that there is an electric region or better, a realm of electricity, of magnetism, of sound, and so on, as there is a kingdom of minerals or plants. Between this hypothesis and the desire to verify it, there is only one step, which these absolute logicians took immediately. But how to perceive these kingdoms of fluidic forces? It was necessary either to find apparatuses sensitive to their action, to expand the power of our senses, or to find a special education for our sensory nervous system. If these brahmins had been pure materialists, they would have sought according to the first method; if they had been simply mystical, they would have chosen the second. But their mode of study consists in reconciling these extremes of materialism and mysticism; they therefore used a mixed method.

Here's how I can explain it to you. Let us take magnetism as an example; they sought to create an artificial magnetic plane, then to know the functions of the magnetic force in man, and finally to bring the two centers together. To create this artificial magnetic plane, they had to draw up tables of variations; they have found the most striking movements of terrestrial magnetism in connection with certain phases of the moon and with certain sunspots.

Moreover, they studied the vibrations of this same force in the body of man, and they found that its center of radiation appeared to be the navel.

You know that the soothsayers of Europe see in their ecstasy, through the solar plexus, or through their fingers; from the psychological point of view it means that the sensory quality of the nervous fluid has been transfused into the nerves of the vegetative life. The brahmins have long known this art of making the nervous system of the great sympathetic conscious; it's a part of what they call yoga. It was therefore easy for them to find a set of exercises to feel and think through the umbilical plexus.

From then on, their enterprise was almost completed. It was only a matter of putting a trained subject in relation to the point in space and the moment when a strong magnetic radiation was to be produced; in this wave, the experimenter would be drawn, would be drawn, observing its movements and effects through a carefully preserved attachment point with the physical plane, could come to have a foothold in the ordinary world while benefiting from a life-threatening surge. So would a diver whose stay in the sea would not be restricted by the necessities of respiration.

When these explanations and many others which I do not reproduce were given to me, I immediately inquired if it would be possible for me to take part in an experiment of this kind. They answered yes in principle, but it was a dangerous thing. The training was long, delicate, and painful; one would risk his cerebral faculties, his health, etc. I replied simply that my instructors would judge my abilities better than I, and we on both sides seemed to forget this project.

However, a few months later, Sankhyananda told me that they had decided to try an experiment of this kind during the winter; we had every reason to foresee for a week at least a few earthquakes on a line that passed through our temples, and we were not sorry, on this occasion, to check some old documents.

They were kind enough to accept me among the five operators. In short, it was a question, according to the principle already stated, of bringing to a given point a large part of the subterranean force being studied. The law which causes the water to flow quite naturally into the basin that is dug for it, also acts for all the forces of Nature, which the brahmins considered substances. The one which concerns us, and which they called the Storm-of-the-Regions-Underground, was to be attracted magnetically by the creation of a pole of an analogous artificial force and of contrary direction.

We therefore had weeks of preliminary training: there were attitudes to keep, words to meditate on and mentally repeat, a special rhythm to give to the breath, and many things more to observe. I do not know what these works give of the real and eternal to the soul, but they procure for man a delicious physical and mental joy; one is young, the senses active, the thought lucid, the understanding clear as a calm lake; things are friendly to you, the serenity of Nature penetrates you; one finds oneself free from worry, from apprehension, from the suffering in which poor human beings struggle.

We began our experiment one afternoon before sunset; we had chosen for that a small circle of rocks, in the vicinity; the leader of the enterprise had us clean the floor; it had been decorated with various figures and letters which expressed the properties of the Storm-Subterranean; the powders, the colors, the perfumes, the woods, the clothes, the orientation were chosen according to what we had believed to discover that was similar to the unknown force among the mineral kingdom, the vegetable, in the plane of the light, of the smells, and the spaces. I was simply told not to move from my place for any reason, even though the ground seemed to open up at my feet. We sat down in places designated in advance, and we entered into one of those psychic states which precede ecstasy and which are called *Dhyana*. I was still aware of the physical plane; I saw my companions; our leader, who, standing and naked a few meters in front of us, was murmuring his mantrams and moving lighted sticks in his hands, while nauseating algae was burning. I also felt myself descending into a dark place, similar to a very old palace; the columns and the inhabitants of this palace made a spot on the horizon, on the stones and the rare trees of the meadow, as in spiritualist photographs one sees the phantom veiling the contours of the furniture. The air also seemed to become drier, and although I could no longer smell the intolerable odor of asafœtida because breathing only takes place in the state I was in about every half-hour, another taste, as the people say, invaded the throat and nostrils. Heavy, greasy, bitter, damp, with sour streaks, this horrible perfume was suddenly accompanied by the enormous sound of muffled thunder, in the center of which we would have found ourselves. All the bones of my body were responding to these deep vibrations; I started to suffer, as when in a nightmare one has the sensation of an endless fall. My leg muscles were contracting involuntarily because my physical body was afraid and wanted to flee; but I knew that to leave the place was death for me and for my companions; one does not expose oneself with impunity to the uncovered rays of the secret forces of the earth.

Add to these anxieties the worry of not knowing what to do, of being dependent on the master: the time I spent there was very unpleasant and seemed very long. Now, while I was trying to stay at my post while falling asleep, I saw a little above our heads two eyes which looked at all five of us at the same time with curiosity, cunning, and a superior feeling of power; a round and immobile head, crowned, took shape; then a body drawn up on one leg, the other folded; sumptuous clothes, unheard-of jewels; only, to the shoulders were attached multiple arms, about twenty perhaps. Two of them were immovable, in front of the chest, making the gesture that lights the magic fire from Below. The others seemed like vibrating waves, so fast did they move. And contemplating this fantastic giant, drawn in black on black, seen in the glow of red lightnings from some of his hands, I had the sensation of an enormous machine to make force, an intelligent machine, alive, but obedient like an antediluvian monster just domesticated; the cold of fear embraced our loins; our marrow froze in this dull and penetrating rumbling. For a moment, I saw the naked body of the master dripping with sweat. The leaves on which we were crouching turned yellow; at this sign we knew that the Presence of the Underground Regions had stopped talking: the whole phantasm appeared under the leaves. appeared, indeed, under the rays of the already high moon. It had been six hours that we had been there, fighting against the intuitive fear, the most terrible of all fears.

The following night, after having slept all day, for my nervous system does not have the power of the Hindus, I recognized that I had taken a great step.

I clearly saw the forces that lead the world reveal themselves little by little according to the measure of the one who looks at them. At first they appear as chance occurrences; then, we discover them in the form of fluids, waves, vibrations; afterwards, long after, we see that they are individual beings. The child who plays the drum is perceived by the learned ant; it builds a system and says: this noise is the result of an undulatory vibration, which arises more particularly around these sorts of continents which rise towards the sky to a dizzying height; it says that or something similar just like an academician. If it goes further, she notices that the noise is produced by a kind of giant smeared with jam, which brandishes chopsticks on a cylinder; it is then the mystic is put in front of one of the inhabitants of the Unknown.

I begin to understand that I don't know anything: I can only experience Life; ah! I wish with all my soul to be able to do that; I feel that you will help me and that thus we will unite more despite the matter, despite the time.

𝒬ETTER XX

THÉOPHANE TO STELLA

My child, be at peace. Soon I will be able to tell you: be happy. Your heart has grown, it has conceived that it could live by itself; that the beauty of your body, a palace, a city, festivals were useless and harmful to the development of its essential power. The strength of your love has brought to your mind some of the mysteries that make up true life. Your love has fought for the one it loves; it saved him from pitfalls, it took upon itself clouds, burdens, rocky paths. You are going to cross the gates of the world of Love, you will have the predominant role there, you will have become one from two beings; Andréas will give you all his thought, you will give him all your Soul; you will be the benefactress, but I can tell you, because true love immolates itself and annihilates itself in the abysses of humility. Both of you will begin to live as one winged, resplendent, immortal being; you will sail on the waves, in the fluid skies of a world of light where the feelings that we call faith, hope, and charity are palpable, nourishing substances; you will incarnate, you will be a molecule of one of those substances of the Sacred Realm of which its palaces are built.

You will be a living, intelligent, blessing stone, adorer of one of the infinities under which the Father reveals himself to his children.

It is here that the first glimmer of eternity shines. The language of men cannot make its brilliance visible. This is why silence becomes necessary, and if we still communicate together from now on, it will be by the ineffable powers of the Spirit.

SEDIR.

www.ingramcontent.com/pod-product-compliance
Lightning Source LLC
Chambersburg PA
CBHW071434090426
42737CB00011B/1656

* 9 781914 166259 *